God,
Why Won't You Talk To Me?

God,

*From Silence
to Hearing
God Every Day*

Why Won't You Talk To Me?

EDWARD L. CARPENTER

For information about this title or to order other books and/or electronic media, contact the publisher:

The Carpenter Ministries, Inc.
thecarpenterministries.com
thecarpenterministries@gmail.com

ISBNs:
978-1-7350126-0-5 (hardcover)
978-1-7350126-1-2 (softcover)
978-1-7350126-2-9 (eBook)

Printed in the United States of America

Cover and Interior design: 1106 Design

CONTENTS

PREFACE

How did it all start?

After weeks of running to different cities, constant stress, and seemingly being pulled in all directions, we finally arrived for the first day of orientation at the Christian law school my oldest daughter would be attending. However, once we arrived, the tension seemed only to increase, because it was not her first-choice law school, and, after weeks of running around, she decided she did not want to even walk in the door. As our argument escalated, it ended with me dropping the F-bomb on my daughter in the middle of the parking lot of this Christian university. In my mind, I saw her face change from the 22-year-old woman in front of me into the 8-year-old little girl I used to cherish. The next thought that ran through my mind was, *How did a self-professed follower of Christ end up at this point?*

At that moment, was I a Christian? Did I honestly believe everything that I had been taught in church during my life? One of the saddest parts is that, right at the very moment this happened, thinking there was no one else around but my daughter and I, I noticed that one of the professors had walked over to us to congratulate us on being accepted to their Christian university.

Strife, anxiety, self-doubt, sexual desires, anger, pleasures, wanting more. These are just some of the things that make up our flesh, our worldly spirit, that rule our minds and bodies before we begin to hear God's voice and let that control our mind and our spirit instead. This book was written as a word from God to give you rest, encouragement, and insight into how lucky we are to be living in a time after Jesus died for us on the cross, so that now we can clearly hear from God.

Whether you have been a Christian for years or are just now considering becoming one, this book is for you. Every thought and desire that makes up our flesh, the things we do and regret the next day, the things we push down and try not to think about, are a part of us. It does not matter how many times you have said you are sorry for them, or how many pastors have prayed over you for them. They are still there because you have to be able to hear God's voice and partner with Him to finally have victory. I guarantee that, by the time you finish this book, you will be at rest, have a clear understanding of what it is to be at peace, and be able to walk with God as your intimate friend. Every verse in this book is written in the *New American Standard Bible* version, which I have found is the closest to the original Greek and Hebrew, unless it is otherwise noted.

Sincerely,
Ed Carpenter

CHAPTER ONE

THE WAR

You are the prize. You are the treasure,
the pearl of the greatest price.

"⁴⁴The Kingdom of heaven is like a treasure hidden in the field, which a man found and hid again; and from joy over it he goes and sells all that he has and buys that field. ⁴⁵Again, the kingdom of heaven is like a merchant seeking fine pearls, ⁴⁶and upon finding one pearl of great value, he went and sold all that he had and bought it."
— MATTHEW 13:44–46

You are the prize, the greatest treasure of God. God is not against you. Jesus shows this in John 3:16, when he says, "For God so loved the world, that He gave His only begotten Son, that whoever believes in Him shall not perish, but have eternal life." Eternal life is something that many people dream of, but what exactly does Jesus mean when he says, "eternal life"? This is answered in John 17:3: "This is eternal life, that they may know You, the only true God, and Jesus Christ whom you have sent." Jesus is telling us that we can have eternal life today, and that we can personally know God and Jesus now. We do not have to wait and ask ourselves whether or not we will go to heaven when we die. This is not why Jesus came. Rather, God sent Jesus to Earth so that we could personally know Him. It is possible, because, by sending Jesus to die on the cross for our sins, it enabled God to give us the gift of the Holy Spirit. God's own spirit is His gift to us, so that we may know Him and the love He has for us.

However, just as God and His spirit are real, so are Satan and his spirit. There is a war going on between God and Satan, a war for your soul. Revelations 12:7–9 reads, "⁷And there was war in heaven. Michael and his angels were waging war with the dragon. The dragon and his angels waged war, ⁸and they were not strong enough, and there was no longer a place found for them in heaven. ⁹And the great dragon was thrown down, the serpent of old who is called the Devil and Satan, who deceives the whole world; he was thrown down to the earth, and his angels were thrown down with him." This war, however, did not end when Satan was cast out of heaven. Instead, Satan set his sights on a new target to prey on and cause pain to God: us.

God and Satan each have a unique way of persuading you to choose whom you want to make your lord. God does it through love and softly guiding you. "He has been very kind and patient, waiting for you to change, but you think nothing of His kindness. Perhaps you do not understand that God is kind to you so you will change your hearts and lives." (Romans

2:4; New Century Version) On the other hand, Satan will try to persuade you with lies and constant pressure, making it feel like you have no other choice but to follow. The battle for your soul is constant and fierce. There is no rest or downtime for your spirit because you are a prize of the greatest value.

If you have never heard of this battle over your soul before, don't worry. It's not your fault, because everyone must be taught this at some point or another. John 1:5 says, "The Light shines in the darkness, and the darkness did not comprehend it." The word "comprehend" in its translation from Greek means "to seize tight hold of, perceive, to grasp something in a forceful manner, to make one's own." We are all born into this world separated from God, having no understanding who He is or what He is like. We are raised on an Earth ruled by Satan, until Christ returns. This means that, unless someone was sent to you by the Holy Spirit, it is close to impossible to have the knowledge and understanding of this battle. The Bible speaks of this in Romans 10:13–15: "[13]Anyone who calls on the Lord will be saved. [14]But before people can ask the Lord for help, they must believe in Him; and before they can believe in Him, they must hear about Him; and for them to hear about the Lord, someone must tell them; [15]and before someone can go and tell them, that person must be sent. It is written, 'How beautiful is the person who comes to bring good news.'" (New Century Version)

Currently, the Devil still has a strong hold on this Earth because his followers, many of whom are unaware that they are following him, speak his thoughts. However, because of what Jesus did on the cross, as soon as someone asks Jesus for help, the Devil has no authority to stop God from intervening. Satan no longer has the authority, but he still has a large influence on this Earth when we choose to give it to him. Psalms 51:5 says, "I was brought into this world in sin. In sin my mother gave birth to me." Sin, at its core, can be defined as doing something other than what the Lord wants you to do. So, if you are hearing a voice that tells you to go against God, does this mean you are hearing from the Devil? There are only three main voices: God, Satan, and you. Among these three, you are the deciding party—you choose whom you want to listen to.

In Deuteronomy 30:19–20, God says, "[19]I call heaven and earth to witness against you today, that I have set before you life and death, the blessing and the curse. So choose life in order that you may live, you and your descendants, [20]by loving the Lord your God, by obeying His voice, and by holding fast to him; for this is your life and the length of your days, that you may live in the land which the Lord swore to your father, to Abraham, Isaac, and Jacob, to give them." Notice in these verses how God specifically says, "by obeying His voice." If we are to obey God's voice and follow His will for our life, then we need first to learn how to hear His voice.

Are you influenced by what you see? By what you hear or how you feel? Do you make decisions based on the circumstances that you are able to see around you? The answer is most likely "Yes." I have spoken to thousands of Christians who do the same. The Devil has somehow switched the words "faith" and "hope" to mean "I hope so" and "Maybe." But rest assured, one thing that is definite is that Jesus took away the sins of the world. "And He Himself is the propitiation for our sins: and not for ours only, but also for those of the whole world." (1 John 2:2). Before God sent Jesus, we were separated from God and unable to hear His voice. Now, there is no barrier between us and God, and everyone can ask Him for help themselves.

Before hearing Christ, all we know, feel, and understand is what the Devil—and the world—have taught us. Ephesians 2:1–3 says, "[1]And you were dead in your trespasses and sins, [2]in which you formerly walked according to the course of this world, according to the prince of power of the air, of the spirit that is now working in the sons of disobedience. [3]Among them we too all formerly lived in the lusts of our flesh, indulging the desires of the flesh and of the mind, and were by nature children of wrath, even as the rest." In these verses, the "prince of power of the air" is Satan, who works through the "sons of disobedience," who is all of the people who choose not to follow God.

Satan uses all of these "sons of disobedience" to influence the world against God. When God created the world, He gave us two trees to choose from. One was for eternal life, and the other was for the knowledge of good and evil. God told Adam and Eve not to eat of the tree of the knowledge of good and evil. The Devil eventually tricked us into eating fruit from the forbidden tree. Because Adam and Eve listened to the Devil and not God, when they ate the forbidden fruit, we became separated from God, and we were no longer one with God. This also allowed the Devil to have influence on us and the world.

It is the same even today, except, because of Jesus dying on the cross, we are now able to learn to hear God's voice once again through His spirit. But until we learn to hear God's voice, all we have is the knowledge of good and evil, and what the Devil has taught us through worldly influences. Every time we use our own knowledge to decide between right and wrong, we are, in our spirits, still eating from the tree of the knowledge of good and evil. This keeps us separated not only from God but also from one another, because every person will always have thoughts and decisions different from others'. These different thoughts, ideas, and decisions are what have grown into different religions and theologies. These different ideologies have caused many conflicts throughout history, but God never meant for us to have the knowledge of good and evil, because we were not designed to be the judge of things—God was. God always wanted us to eat from the tree of eternal life, which is listening to, and learning from, God personally. God is a spirit, so the love that He gives to people is also spiritual.

Before we find God and learn to hear His voice, we are in a world that is ruled by the Devil, and our mind, body, and spirit only know what we have been taught and how it makes our body or emotions feel. If it feels good to us, then it must be good. If it profits us, then it must be a sign to go in that direction. Even when it comes to picking a religion to follow, the same ideas apply: What feels good to us, and how does it profit us? Humans pick from hundreds of religions to follow:

Atheist, Buddhist, Muslim, various Christian denominations, Latter-Day Saints, etc. Why is this? Why are there so many different religions in the world? Simply put, it is because we are all still being filled with the knowledge of good and evil. Satan teaches the world—and, therefore, us—when we do not know God, that the concept of what "good" is depends on whether it feels good and benefits us. It's the same with many of the world's religions, religions that humans created to give them a definition of what "good" is. Humans have created hundreds of religions to justify what we *deem* good, rather than going to the source of what good *is*: God.

Once we have set in our minds what is "good," anytime we see someone not fall in line with that definition, we consider them to be "bad." Again, this is us playing the role of judge, which is a role we were never meant to be cast in. When we see people constantly going against what we deem "good," whether or not those people do not see their actions as such, it is often decided that they need to be stopped. This can escalate all the way into war in order to make those doing "bad" deeds stop. This knowledge of good and bad has been so corrupted by the Devil that we often have no idea what their true meaning is. Even in today's world, which teaches us to accept everything and everyone, as soon as someone expresses that they do not believe in certain things, those who supposedly "accept everything and everyone" suddenly turn to hate and chastise those who do not fully agree with them.

Out of everything God created for us in the Garden of Eden, God gave us only one rule: Do not eat fruit from the tree of knowledge of good and evil. But Adam and Eve did it anyway, and because our ancestors chose to do this, we are born with this sin as well. Every day, in almost everything, we decide what is right or wrong for us, based on how the Devil has taught us to decide and how it makes us feel. An example of this can be seen when the teachers of the bible tried to prove what they new about God's word to Jesus. Jesus showed the teachers of the bible that it's not just about using the word of God to correct people. But it's about hearing the Spirit of God reveal to you which scripture to use at the precise moment.

"³The scribes and the Pharisees brought a woman caught in adultery, and having set her in the center of the court, ⁴they said to Him, 'Teacher, this woman has been caught in adultery, in the very act. ⁵Now in the Law Moses commanded us to stone such women; what then do You say?' ⁶They were saying this, testing Him, so that they might have grounds for accusing Him. But Jesus stooped down and with His finger wrote on the ground. ⁷But when they persisted in asking Him, He straightened up, and said to them, 'He who is without sin among you, let him be first to throw a stone at her.' ⁸Again He stooped down and wrote on the ground. ⁹When they heard it, they began to go out one by one, beginning with the older ones, and He was left alone, and the woman, where she was, in the center of the court. ¹⁰Straightening up, Jesus said to her, 'Woman, where are they? Did no one condemn

you?' ¹¹She said, 'No one, Lord.' And Jesus said, 'I do not condemn you, either. Go. From now on sin no more.'"
—JOHN 8:3–11

In these verses, the Pharisees were looking at their world with what they thought was right and wrong. Even though they were basing their decision on the black-and-white law of Moses, it was no longer correct, because that is what God sent Jesus to Earth to change. Now, after Jesus died on the cross, we no longer have to rely on the black-and-white law of the Old Testament. Rather we can now hear directly from God, just as in the story above. When pressure is put on us to make a decision, we can take a moment, like Jesus did, to hear from God. The first black-and-white scripture you find will not always be the correct one. You have to hear from God yourself. This is why God sent Jesus to the Earth.

However, oftentimes, we do not act like Jesus did. Life teaches us to have no mercy for anyone who breaks our standards. Instead, we hold a grudge. However, while holding others to an almost perfect standard, we tend to have a large amount of grace for ourselves when we make mistakes. This is because when people make a mistake, they tend to justify it with the circumstances and facts leading up to the mistake, justifying the action and changing the standard for the next time a similar circumstance arises. Or sometimes we can find ourselves saying, "Well, I'm just a human. I'm going to make mistakes." And yet, when someone *else* makes the same mistake, we will hold it against them. On the other side of this coin is when we give *everyone* totally free grace, allowing them to trample on others and on ourselves. This was seen with the hippy freedom in the '60s and is starting to be seen again in today's society. This is when we become so afraid of upsetting someone that we allow them to do and believe whatever they decide is their "truth." This is still the Devil's ideology, because it continues to push the wrong definitions of love and truth. In the Bible, it says that God is love, and because He is love, then we must listen to Him in order to know what real love is.

Take a moment to ask yourself: Are you at peace? Has what you believed really been working for you? Something I taught my three daughters growing up was that occasionally we all need to have a "coming to Jesus" moment where we ask ourselves if what we are doing is really working for us. An example of this would be telling yourself that having sex with each person you go on a date with is fine, because this next person will stay and love you unconditionally. However, eventually, we all have to have the "coming to Jesus" moment, where we wake up and realize that this is not working. We have to go and hear from God ourselves how to fix the situation and what the real truth is. Romans 8:28 reads, "And we know that God causes all things to work together for good to those who love God, to those who are called according to His purpose." This means that, as we align ourselves with God and step onto the road that He has created for us in this life, He will make the path straight for us to walk on, and things will begin to work for good in our lives.

In order to achieve this, we have to be honest with ourselves about our choices and lives. It can often be painful to sit and think about our mistakes and bad habits truthfully. Some people also feel that, if they are honest with themselves, then God will be upset. But it is actually the opposite! God *wants* us to have these moments, so that we can start to see how the enemy has put us into spiritual bondage, keeping us from doing things that will bring us closer to God. Spiritual bondage can be hard to pinpoint at first, but ask yourself: *Am I able to control my own spirit? Am I able to control my mind and spirit to keep my body from doing things that I know I will regret the next day?* Proverbs 16:32 says, "He who is slow to anger is better than the mighty, and he who rules his spirit, than he who captures a city." It is close to impossible to have control over our flesh and spirit without God. Only God's spirit speaking to us can get us to the better "dream" life we have been desiring. Next time something happens that you know is going to cause regret later on, think about the reasons why you did it. Oftentimes you will find excuses to do it, such as: "I didn't want to lose face with my peers." Or "It was only this one time, and life is short." This is not you—*or* your thoughts. Rather, it is the enemy pushing you to move further and further from God.

While this can be painful to fully realize, it is a good thing. Once you realize this, you are on your way to freedom. This struggle between God's spirit and our worldly flesh and spirit is best expressed in Romans 7:14–25 (New Century Version), which reads,

"*[14]We know that the law is spiritual, but I am not spiritual since sin rules me as if I were its slave. [15]I do not understand the things I do. I do not do what I want to do, and I do the things I hate.* [16]*And if I do not want to do the hated things I do, that means I agree that the law is good.* [17]*But I am not really the one who is doing these hated things; it is sin living in me that does them.* [18]*Yes, I know that nothing good lives in the part of me that is earthly and sinful. I want to do the things that are good, but I do not do them.* [19]*I do not do the good things I want to do, but I do the bad things I do not want to do.* [20]*So if I do things I do not want to do, then I am not the one doing them. It is sin living in me that does those things.* [21]*So I have learned this rule: When I want to do good, evil is there with me.* [22]*In my mind, I am happy with God's law.* [23]*But I see another law working in my body, which makes way against the law that my mind accepts. That other law working in my body is the law of sin, and it makes me its prisoner.* [24]*What a miserable man I am! Who will save me from this body that brings me death?* [25]*I thank God for saving me through Jesus Christ our Lord! So in my mind I am a slave to God's law, but in my sinful self, I am a slave to the law of sin."*

Remember: You are the prize of greatest worth, and God sent Christ to free you from all your wrong thoughts and actions.

CHAPTER TWO

GOD *IS* LOVE

*Understanding the full extent
of God's love for YOU.*

Before you can begin to fully hear God's voice and walk in peace, you must first be able to trust Him. As we discussed in Chapter 1, everyone, before they find Christ, starts out with only worldly knowledge, which, again, is the fallen world ruled by the Devil. We must first establish a true and Biblical base to build upon when it comes to choosing to believe in God.

First, or mainly, you must believe that *God Is Love*. It sounds simple enough, right? If any Christian were asked if they believed God was love, they would most likely answer "Yes." However, oftentimes, while they answered "Yes," deep down, they still believe that God is out to punish us. Evidence of this is when we say, "Boy, God is mad at us" when disasters such as tornadoes and hurricanes strike. Or if someone is sick, they think that it is God's doing and that He must be using it to teach them something. Another example is if their business is failing. God must be mad at them.

A common, but incorrect, thinking in the church is that, if someone is not tithing, or if there is a sin in their life, God will punish them with earthly things like those listed above. The incorrect focus on God punishing believers for not living the "perfect" Christian life shifts the focus from God being love and wanting to bless you—and Satan being the one that wants to kill, steal, and destroy—to God being right alongside the Devil in wanting to make life a living hell. This is *not* correct! Satan would love nothing more than to trick believers into thinking that God is here only to punish us. It's a common lie that the Devil has pushed on the world, through TV, radio—and even through world religions—since the very beginning.

This kind of thinking must be addressed if we want to have a successful relationship with God. Think about it: On Earth, how do we have a successful relationship? Communication, honesty, and openness are some of the most important aspects of Earthly relationships with each other, and they are also some of the most important aspects of having a successful relationship with God. We need to be able to put our whole trust in God, which can be hard enough when we cannot physically see Him. If someone is thinking that God is out to punish them, how can they be expected to put their whole trust into a punisher?

Take a moment and think deeply to yourself. Do you believe that God is purely love, wanting what is best for you, celebrating when you celebrate, and crying when you cry? That He wants only peace, prosperity, health, happiness, love, and success for you? Or do you carry a fear that, if you decide to give your life completely to God, there will be something—a habit, action, or physical object—He is going to take away from you?

It is another common lie and strategy of the Devil to feed into the world that our Creator, God, is there only to take things away from us rather than bless us with gifts—or that He is withholding things from us that we would enjoy. This is something that every Christian will struggle with at some point during their walk of faith. Let's look at Genesis. It is set in the Garden of Eden, God's creation for us. Everything is perfect for and with mankind. God made Adam and Eve, and gave them rule over the Earth. This is part of the reason that, in today's world, God cannot just come in and fix everything and make it perfect. He has already given authority over the world to us, and it is now up to us to work with God and use that authority or to keep handing the keys over to the Devil by walking in the ways of the world. In the Garden, God placed two special trees. One was the tree of life; if they ate from it, they would receive eternal life. The other tree was the tree of the knowledge of good and evil. God told them that, if they ate from this tree, they would surely die, and not to eat of it.

As I said earlier, Satan has been using the same tricks since the very beginning, trying to convince humanity that God is out to get them and withhold good things from them. In Genesis 3, Satan came to Eve with this exact same lie—that God was keeping something desirable from her, the knowledge of good and evil. Now, Eve had seen God and used to take walks in the Garden with him. Yet she believed, and even agreed with the Devil, that God was keeping good things from her.

This is one of many examples of how persuasive and sneaky the devil and the ways of the world are. They will promise you everything, only to end up empty when you arrive. It is a constant temptation to want the things of the world; our flesh craves it. However, the more time we spend with God, the more our spirit can easily overrule our flesh. Eve was perfect; she had no sin in her, until she believed that what the Devil was telling her was truth and that what God had told her was not. Her belief in the word of the Devil over the word of God was the sin. It was not the action of eating the fruit, but rather the action and intent in her heart with which the sin was acted on.

As I briefly explained above, this is how we live today. We are spiritual beings; our body acts on what our mind chooses to believe. We cannot escape this. All our actions are based on beliefs—either those of the world, aka the Devil, or of God. When Eve chose the Devil over God, sin entered the world, handing the authority God had given us over the world to Satan, allowing him to influence everything you see around you. God, being completely perfect and made fully of goodness, could not be around sin and all the carnal desires that come with it. Because of this, we were separated from His presence. Humans choose to distance themselves from God, which only gives the Devil more and more lordship over the Earth.

When looking in the Bible, and in God's truth, it is revealed that there is no truth in the Devil and that he is exclusively here to kill, steal, and destroy us. Yet, many often fall for the thought that maybe there is a little truth in the thought that our worldly desires are not all that bad. Without having the

Holy Spirit in us, there is, literally, no right thinking in humans at all. Without God, we are born into sin, raised by sin, and look at everything through the eyes of sin.

> *"⁹What then? Are we better than they? Not at all; for we have already charged that both Jews and Greeks are all under sin; ¹⁰as it is written, "There is none righteous, not even one; ¹¹there is none who understands, there is none who seeks for God; ¹²all have turned aside, together they have become useless; there is no one who does good, there is not even one."*
>
> —ROMANS 3:9–12

Remember, this book was written to teach you how to hear from God, who is love and wants what is best for you. All of the harsh realities of the ways of the world discussed above were written to help you realize that you have grace for your incorrect beliefs and mistakes. Think of your spirit as a garden. If your garden is full of weeds, or lies from the enemy, then no good fruit can grow. However, as the weeds are uprooted and removed, there is more room for beautiful flowers and healthy, fruit-producing trees to grow. There is more room for God's perfect and complete truth to take seed and develop in your spirit. Eve was created *perfect*, and yet even she was still deceived. Our whole world is lost and deceived, and looks at everything, including the Bible, through a lens of lies of the enemy. This is not to say that Christians make mistakes only when they are deceived by the Devil. Eve was deceived, but

Adam was not. He ate of the fruit knowing exactly what he was doing was wrong. That is even worse—knowingly going against God with the intent of doing exactly that. However, so often Christians—each and every day—walk straight into sin knowing exactly what they are doing is completely against God.

Because of Adam and Eve's sin, we needed grace. We had no hope of knowing the truth, and God could not reach us because we were consistently choosing to believe in the Devil and trusting in his worldly knowledge, causing us to look at everything through the lens of sin. From the first sin on Earth—Adam and Eve eating from the forbidden tree—we gained the knowledge of good and evil. From this, we began to judge anything and everything based on our worldly knowledge. We were not created to have this knowledge, and this knowledge is what is causing so much strife and hardship in today's world. Think about it: Worldwide, how many different "truths" are there? It is a common phrase to hear someone say, "Well, this is *my* truth." The Devil encourages this, causing humanity to fall further and further from the *actual* truth, found only in God. How many times have you judged someone to make yourself feel better? Or compared your actions to someone who had done worse to justify yourself? We often will justify ourselves of this action because of all the circumstances that led up to it, however, this is a vicious cycle that never ends. We hate, judge, do the same thing, hate, judge, do the same thing, etc.

The only way to break the cycle is to realign with real truth, which is God's truth. However, in order to do this, we need to be free from the rule of the Devil and the authority he has over the Earth. Remember that God is made completely of love, and when we choose to walk away from Him, it breaks His heart, because He knows how we can be hurt by the world when we are not in relationship with him. So, from the moment sin entered the world, God set into place a plan that would redeem our faults and sins, so that we could be in relationship with God once again.

This plan entered the world as His son, Jesus Christ. Because of Christ's sacrifice on the cross, we are freed from the power of Satan over us when we believe in, and walk with, God. This separation—of choosing to serve God over worldly desires—can be seen in Romans 7:25: "Thanks be to God through Jesus Christ our Lord! So then, on the one hand I myself with my mind am serving the law of God, but on the other, with my flesh the law of sin."

So how do we access this freedom? By having a relationship with God. The path to freedom is not through simply believing. Many Christians will say they believe in God but will continue to walk in their ways of sin, knowing it is directly against God's truth. It needs to be more than that. We must have a relationship with God, to trust Him and His truth. We must believe that it is truly what is best for us, and that God is not withholding any good from us when we choose to give up our sinful actions and instead choose to follow God's truth. But as I discussed earlier in this chapter, you must have communication in order to have a successful relationship, whether it be here on Earth or spiritually with God. You need to hear God's voice speak to you, instead of the voice of the world.

Please understand that it is God, and only God, who made the way for us to have a relationship with Him. There was nothing we could have done in order to right the wrong of sin and achieve perfection to be in His presence. No amount of work or good deeds would accomplish this. It was only by God sending His son to die on the cross that we were able to once again walk with God.

It was, and still is, all God. God is hope; this is something that is repeated a lot within the church, but it is true! Before Jesus, there was no hope in the world—no hope for the next day or for what comes after life.

"¹²Remember that you were at that time separate from Christ, excluded from the commonwealth of Israel, and strangers to the covenants of promise, having no hope and without God in the world. ¹³But now in Christ Jesus you who formerly were far off have been brought near by the blood of Christ."
—**EPHESIANS 2:12–13**

When reading this verse in today's world, it is easy to brush it off, saying, "Well, I am not a part of the 'commonwealth of Israel' anyway." But this verse is not speaking of the literal, Earthly version of Israel, but instead is referring to the spiritual representation of it as God's chosen people. Those who believe and commune with Him each and every day are counted as His children. Humans were not the first ones to reach back out to God. Why would we? We were lost in the worldly ways, thinking that we would have to give up all of our fun in order to be "perfect." But there is no way for us to be perfect—not within our own strength. Instead, the only way to be able to freely come before God as His children is through God's son, Jesus Christ.

> *"¹³When you were dead in your transgressions and the uncircumcision of your flesh, He made you alive together with Him, having forgiven us of all our transgressions, ¹⁴having cancelled out the certificate of debt consisting of decrees against us, which was hostile to us; and He has taken it out of the way, having nailed it to the cross."*
> —COLOSSIANS 2:13–14

Every Christian knows that they were saved because of Jesus Christ, so why repeat it? Because before His sacrifice, we were unable to hear from God. There are other books, such as *The Power of the Blood,* by Andrew Murray, that go deeper into this particular subject. However, in order to begin hearing God's voice, we simply need to know that Jesus, sent by God, restored our ability to hear God through the Holy Spirit. From there, we can dive deeper into everything that Christ's sacrifice did for us, with books like the one mentioned above, and through God speaking to us and teaching us Himself.

Understand this: as far as God is concerned, there is no more sin separating you from His presence the moment you believe in Him. Praise the Lord! So why do we still have so much trouble and temptation in our lives? Think back, to earlier in the chapter, when I mentioned how God gave us the keys of authority over the world, found in Genesis 1:26, "Let us make man in our image, according to our likeness; and let them rule over the fish of the sea and over the birds of the sky and over the cattle and over all the earth, and over every creeping thing that creeps on the earth." It was not just Adam and Eve; we still hold the keys of authority today, and we have a seemingly huge uphill battle ahead of us. Unlike Adam and Eve, we have been conditioned from birth to have our thinking filled with falsehood, and our bodies are conditioned to agree with that falsehood.

A perfect example is when nighttime comes. You may not want to go out and party, you may not want to sleep around, you may not want to get high, but your body forces you. Your thoughts override what you feel deep inside. The feeling of *not* wanting to go out and party or do any of the things mentioned above is the Spirit of God. Any thought or feeling deep inside of you that is actively fighting to not do any of the things mentioned above, along with other worldly desires, is from the Spirit of God. Nothing innately in our human flesh would say "No" to making the flesh feel good. It is God trying to speak to you and gently guide you to His truth. And yet, oftentimes we ignore this small voice, go and do what pleases our flesh, and then feel guilty the next day, as the same spirit that seemingly forces you to go out and party is now telling you what a horrible person you are. This voice that makes you feel guilty for everything is not God—it is the Devil. The Devil will make sin seem like the best thing in the world. Then, as soon as you step into the sin, he immediately changes his tune to "How could you?" or "I cannot believe you did this again"!

But praise the Lord Jesus! Through His sacrifice, the freedom to break from this bondage is given to us. But this can be done only by hearing his voice. If you read the Bible, realize what you've been doing is wrong, and want to change, know that without hearing God's voice, you will fail. It's not just you, but rather every single Christian who has ever walked the Earth. Some preachers have teachings that can get you motivated to walk more in line with God, which is, at its core, a good thing. However, some preachers then continue on, saying that you can do it with your sheer willpower, which causes people to start fighting against the sin with their own mind and body. This will not work. As I mentioned above, it is only through God that we are redeemed of our sins, and it is only through Him that we can be freed from them. There is no amount of effort or work we can do to achieve this without direct help from God.

If we try to work independently from God, to accomplish things in this world with our own strength, even if it is getting rid of sinful habits, it is still considered a sin. This is because we are separating ourselves from God, becoming independent from Him, in order to accomplish the very thing we need His help with. This can be seen in Romans 14:23: *"But he who doubts is condemned if he eats, because his eating is not from faith; **and whatever is not from faith is sin.**"* If we try to use our own strength, it is basically telling God that we do not

23

need Him, and that we can do it ourselves, which is rebelling against Him.

So, how do we hear God's voice? How can we be like King David when he wrote in Psalms 119:105, "God's word is a lamp to my feet, and light to my path." It can be as simple as listening to that little voice, mentioned earlier, telling you not to go out and party, get high, or indulge in other worldly activities. The more you listen to that little voice that lines up with what the Bible says, the stronger it will become. However, it becomes easier and easier to hear His voice the more you clear a path for Him in your spirit. Clearing a path toward God's voice simply means coming to terms with His unyielding love for you, along with several other truths about who God is that we will discuss in further chapters of this book.

In summary, you must begin to learn that God loves you. God's love is not like the flawed human love we see here on Earth, where you have to act a certain way to be loved. God's love is unconditional. God loves you no matter what, and He will never love you any more or any less, no matter how you act. He is overjoyed with you. You are His child! He is our father, unlike any Earthly father we have seen. His love is perfect; you do not have to work to earn His favor. You do not have to be afraid of His punishments. You do not ever have to be afraid that He will leave you. He wants what is truly best for you and wants to bless you.

Humanity was separated from God as soon as sin entered the world, and everyone since then has been born into sin and raised in sin, not hearing God, doing and believing everything

Satan tells us. We have been saved from this! Even while you were living fully for the world, God loved you fully and completely, just as much as He loves you now. God came and rescued us through His son, Jesus Christ, who died on the cross for us, perfect and without sin. Jesus died in our place. The strongest foundation to build your faith and walk with God on through life is the realization of just how much God loves you. And the main cornerstone is Jesus. We did nothing ourselves, and we would have never been able to; God did it all through His only begotten Son, Jesus.

Below are some verses, or words of God, to meditate on and put inside your mind, heart, and spirit. The more we focus on the words of God, the more they will grow inside of us and start to push out of the lies of Satan.

Romans 9:33 *"Just as it is written, 'Behold, I lay in Zion a stone of stumbling and a rock of offense, and he who believes in Him will not be disappointed.'"*

Isaiah 28:16 *"Therefore thus says the Lord God, 'Behold, I am laying in Zion a stone, a tested stone, a costly cornerstone for the foundation firmly placed. He who believes in it will not be disturbed.'"*

1 Peter 2:7–8 *"⁷This precious value, then, is for you who believe, 'The stone which the builders rejected, this became the very cornerstone,' ⁸and, 'A stone of stumbling and a rock of offense'; for they stumble because they are* *disobedient to the word, and to this doom they were also appointed.*"

Acts 4:11–12 "¹¹*He is the stone which was rejected by you, the builders, but which became the chief cornerstone.* ¹²*And there is salvation in no one else; for there is no other name under heaven that has been given among men by which we must be saved.*"

Psalms 118:22–24 "²²*The stone which the builders rejected has become the chief cornerstone.* ²³*This is the Lord's doing; It is marvelous in our eyes.* ²⁴*This is the day which the Lord has made; Let us rejoice and be glad in it.*"

CHAPTER THREE

TAKE A TEST DRIVE

Taste and see that God is good

As I mentioned in the previous chapter, to genuinely believe in God and hear His voice, you first need to learn and believe that He is good. You need to learn that God is here to help you and wants what is best for you. However, in order to learn and believe that He is good, we must hear His voice to encourage and teach us. While this seems like a problem with no solution, I promise that there is an easy solution.

Every Christian unknowingly hears God's voice throughout their lives but don't recognize it as God's until they choose to grow closer to Him. They don't recognize God speaking to them because they are not accustomed to it. Think about it like this: If you are out in public and a close friend or family member calls out to you, you recognize who is speaking to you, right? However, if you are in public and a stranger calls out, how likely are you to miss that they were talking to you? It's the same with hearing the voice of God. I guarantee that

He has spoken to you before, but because you are not in a close relationship with Him, you missed it.

Let's go through some of the instances where you could have heard His voice and not recognized it. Often, it's not an audible voice, but rather a feeling or a thought. Remember that, before we become Christians and are born again, we are made fully of flesh and of the world, which is full of the knowledge that Satan pushes on people every day. I remind you of this, because, in our fleshly knowledge, we will often write off the different ways in which God has spoken to us. However, once we can pinpoint those moments, we can begin to meditate on that, and our ability to hear God's voice will grow.

No doubt, you've gotten to a point in your life where you feel that you can't stop doing things; even though, in your mind, you *want* to stop, your body just seems to continue without your consent. You try and try again to break a bad habit and are unable to. Immediately, Satan will start putting thoughts in your mind such as: "Hey, maybe this is just the way I was created." Or "What's the point of struggling with this anymore, when I could just give in?" But deep down, you still seem to have this fire to be better, knowing you were created for more than this. *That* is God's voice. Those deep thoughts and feelings that encourage you to keep going, to keep fighting for something better, is God reaching out to you.

Praise the Lord that Jesus Christ can bypass all the external noise and distractions that Satan and the world place on us. The Holy Spirit can come, live inside of you, and speak directly to you. Even while Satan tries to tempt you away and distract you with his Earthly knowledge, God is right there next to you, waiting for the moment you turn and look to see who is calling out.

As you read this, you may be thinking to yourself, "Well, sure, God sent Jesus and the disciples heard from God, but that's not for us in today's world." Recognize the enemy's voice! Satan will tell you anything he can to keep you from recognizing the call of your heavenly father. Habakkuk 2:14 reads, "For the earth will be filled with the knowledge of the glory of the Lord as the waters cover the sea." We still have oceans and seas today, right? Just as water still covers the sea today, so does the knowledge of the glory of God fill this Earth. The time is now to learn of the glory of God and all the good He wants for you.

Jesus Christ came to this Earth and died on the cross so that the Holy Spirit could come close enough to call out amidst the world's distractions. This is why, in the small, quiet moments away from the noise of the day, whether it be in the middle of the day or before bed, you believe that there is something more. And there is! These thoughts are God's spirit drawing you closer to Him. John 6:44: "For you cannot come to Him unless the Father draws you." God is drawing you toward Him, just as He draws everyone else. God speaks to you through your spirit, and He sent His spirit to the Earth to be with you and to guide you through life. This is what Jesus was referring to when, right before He ascended into heaven, He said, "But the Helper, the Holy Spirit, whom the Father will send in my name. He will teach you all things and remind you of everything I have told you." (John 14:26)

Once you recognize that the deep inner voice or feeling is God speaking to you, His voice will become stronger and stronger. God loves you immensely and wants the best for you. Do not get caught in the Devil's lies about right and wrong. God has made it so simple for us to get to know Him. He gifted us with the Holy Spirit to save us from our troubles and fears. Psalms 34:8 says, "O taste and see that the Lord is good; blessed is the man who takes refuge in Him!" Notice that this verse does not say, "Fall to your knees, repent, accept Christ, and then you will experience the goodness of the Lord." It does not even say that you must accept Christ, but rather to just try a taste of God, and you will see that He is good.

Now, when hearing that God will let you experience Him without first being a Christian, some people say that this is blasphemy. But think about the life of Jesus. He healed and performed miracles on those who did not yet believe that He was the son of God. During His journey, amidst all the healings, miracles, and teachings, the Pharisees were against Him, believing that He was committing blasphemy and speaking out against God. "But woe to you, scribes and Pharisees, hypocrites! Because you shut off the kingdom of heaven before men. For you neither enter, nor even do you allow those who are entering to go in." (Matthew 23:13) Pharisees still exist in today's world and are known as pastors and teachers. If they do not hear God's voice and walk with the Holy Spirit, then they are like the Pharisees, stuck in the written law and against anything that may challenge their tradition. They speak of many rules and roadblocks that can make you believe that it's impossible to reach and have a relationship with God. However, as we've discussed previously, we know that this isn't true and that God is always trying to reach out to us.

Remember how much God loves you! One scripture that best expresses how much God loves every single person in the world is Matthew 5:44–45:

> *"'⁴⁴Remember we are learning about God and His love.' Jesus says 'But I say to you, love your enemies and pray for those who persecute you, ⁴⁵so that you may be sons of your Father who is in heaven; for He causes His sun to rise on the evil and the good, and sends rain on the righteous and the unrighteous.'"*
>
> —MATTHEW 5:44–45

This scripture is talking about how God sends the rain to every person in the world, good or bad, believers and unbelievers, so that they have food to eat and keep their physical bodies healthy. Do you not think that He would do the same for our spiritual bodies—which, to Him, are more important? This is why His spirit cuts through all the outside-world noise to speak to you directly, from the inside of your spirit. In life, we test-drive cars before we buy one. God is the same, loving us so much that He allows us to "test drive" His goodness before we "buy," or put our faith in, Him. He lets us realize how much better His ways are before we decide to fully jump in.

If, at this point, you agree that, deep down, you feel that things should be different or better, but you don't know what to do with it or how to take the first step to see if what the Lord and I have been telling you is true, *keep reading.* Once you realize that God is always trying to reach out to you, it becomes easier to taste and see God's love working through you by His Spirit. If a thought or feeling deep inside you comes to mind, and you realize that it could help you, what's the first thing that happens? Normally, right after this thought or feeling comes from your spirit into your mind, the first thing many people do is think of a million reasons why this is not possible. It becomes a battle of that one thought from deep within you versus all the world's reasons why it can never happen. Essentially it becomes a battle of God versus the Devil.

If you don't recognize that this is God talking to you, it's extremely easy to just brush this feeling or idea off, mainly because of fear. Remember that fear is from the Devil. The thought or feeling that is so easily brushed off by fear or worldly knowledge—yet keeps coming up again and again from deep inside of you—is from God, and it takes faith to believe and act upon it. This realization brings all the scriptures that talk about the fight between faith and fear to life, because that same fight is happening to every single person in today's world.

Your struggle is not on the outside in this life, but, rather, the real battle to win is inside of you, between God and the Devil, a battle in which *you* decide the outcome. Will you act on faith, on God's spoken word deep inside of you? Or will you act out of fear, out of all of the world's reasons why this is impossible, out of the Devil's logic, which keeps you from acting in faith? Most people have this struggle for their entire life. They know something deep down is trying to guide them, but they let fear keep them from doing it. But if you believe what is written in this book, then you have the knowledge that this is actually *God* speaking to you. When you feel or hear this deep inner voice telling you something, ask it to show you an example out of the Bible. God's voice will never contradict what is written in the Bible, simply because He also wrote it! It's OK to use your computer to search what you are hearing to see if it appears in the Bible anywhere. Once you find it, then you have something physical to stand on. This is now where you can lay it all on the line. Just pray, "God, if this is your voice speaking to me, I will act on what I believe is you." And then when it comes to past, you can know that it was the voice of the Lord speaking to you.

Fear is a strong opponent. You cannot beat it on your own. However, when you step out in faith because of what God is telling you, it takes the pressure and blame off of you. It is no longer up to how much work or effort *you* put in to make it happen. Instead it is up to God, and you can rest easy in that. Remember that it is all God—He wants you to lean on, and trust in, Him. He loves showing you His power and strength. King David understood this and spoke of it often in the Psalms. Psalms 3:8 reads, "Salvation belongs to the Lord, Thy blessings upon Thy people!" Basically, whatever that deep feeling or idea is telling you, see if it lines up with the Bible, and, if it does, trust in God to make it happen rather than relying on your own strength and worldly knowledge to do it. It really is that easy.

The next thing that will happen, and it happens without you realizing it, is your spirit will begin to battle against God's spirit. It often seems like you are just talking to yourself. But think about it: God created you, and He created you to communicate with Him. God meets us where we are, and His voice will sound similar to the way you talk and think to yourself, but it will have a different pitch to it. At first, it is difficult to distinguish the difference, but I will cover how to do this later on. For now, understand that a battle is about to take place inside of you. It is a fight for your eternal soul and the peace you long for in this world. Earlier, we discussed how, from birth, we are filled with the world's knowledge, from the Devil, until we choose to communicate with God. This lifetime of worldly training will try to stop you from listening to God because what He is telling you is too different from anything you grew up knowing. Do not worry, though, because, by this point, God already has His foot in the door. You are communicating with Him. The real question is: How long you are going to keep up this fight?

The next way you will know God is speaking to you is it will be hard to say out loud what the inner voice is telling you, even if you are by yourself. It's hard to speak it out loud because of the strong spiritual fight you are in. This battle is the real world you currently do not see with the natural eye. Once you act on what God is telling you, you will feel God's peace breaking through that fear and you will realize what a demonic attack you were under and just how real the spiritual world is. This is the reason Jesus came—to enable the Holy Spirit to come inside of us, giving us the power to overcome.

Now, once you get the courage to speak what God is telling you out loud, even when you are all alone, you are on your way to victory. Let's pause for a moment and focus on what happened when you spoke it out loud. You chose to believe the voice and overcame the first struggle of even saying it out loud, choosing God's will above the world's. Many people believe that every choice and decision they make is by their own will. But this is not true. The Devil has put so many of his lies into this world that people are actually doing everything according to his influences.

As a reminder, the first two big steps or hurdles in learning to recognize God's voice are: 1) You get a thought that is outside of what you normally think, one of success and victory, and 2) Your brain gives you a million reasons why this is not possible, but that little voice keeps coming back, again and again. However, there is a third hurdle that you will eventually encounter and learn to recognize. When you physically go to act on what God has told you, your actual body, or flesh, will directly fight against it. Remember that fear is from the Devil. When you go to step out and act on what God has told you, the Devil will use fear that is different from any fear you have ever felt before as a last-ditch effort to keep you from doing the will of God here on Earth. This fear is almost like a force field that hits you. You are literally going to be so afraid you're going to want to run and hide, but take courage! When you act on that little voice inside of you, it will literally crush the demonic fear you're currently feeling. That's how powerful that small still voice inside of you is. The devil does not want you acting on God's voice inside of you. He is more afraid of God's word than anything else.

These three steps or hurdles are almost always the same. If you have already accepted Jesus as your Lord, you already know these three hurdles well. Do you remember how afraid you were to say out loud that you accepted Christ as your Lord and Savior? By continuing from that day with accepting Jesus, to listening and responding to what God is telling you, you line up with Colossians 2:6–7, which states, "⁶Therefore as you have received Christ Jesus as Lord, so continue to walk in Him, ⁷having been firmly rooted and now being built up in Him and established in your faith, just as you were instructed and overflowing with gratitude."

Again, the first step is simply understanding that the deep-down feeling or voice is God and this is how you begin to hear from God yourself. Hebrews 3:15 says, "Today if you hear his voice, do not harden your hearts as when they provoked me." The word "harden" in the verse means "obstinately stubborn," "resisting" what God says. But what led up to this verse? Who was God referencing as an example for us? If you backtrack to earlier, in Hebrews 3, it is explained.

"⁷Therefore, just as the Holy Spirit says, today if you hear His voice, ⁸do not harden your hearts (Sound familiar?) *as when they provoked me as in the day of trial in the*

*wilderness. ⁹Where your fathers tried me by testing me and saw my works for forty years. ¹⁰Therefore, I was angry with this generation, and said "They always go astray in their heart; and they did not know my ways"; ¹¹as I swore in my wrath, they shall not enter my rest. ¹²Take care, brethren, lest there should be in any one of you an evil unbelieving heart, in falling away from the living God. ¹³But encourage one another day after day, as long as it is still called Today, lest anyone of you be hardened by the deceitfulness of sin. ¹⁴For we have become partakers of Christ, if we hold fast the beginning of our assurance firm until the **end**."*

—HEBREWS 3:7–14

Take note of the word "end," boldfaced in this verse. It does not mean the end of time, or until you die. It means something like the end of the view of a pirate's telescope. You can see far off what God is saying to you through His Spirit; you just need to believe it and watch it come closer and closer into view, into reality.

So, have you made Christ your Savior? If you have not, now is as good a time as any. Say out loud, "Jesus, I need you to be my Lord." For now, just believing that God is for you and wants to help you is enough. Don't get mentally caught up thinking you have to change morally. Jesus took away your sins and now Jesus will help you to do the things you need to do to have peace, but you have to hear from Him. Do not try to do what *you* think is the right way, because it is all muddled in the confusion of this world's logic. You need the pure source of truth and righteousness for yourself. Remember that God did it all—you simply heard Him and let Him lead you inside your heart. You may *think* it is your mind right now and that you gave God the chance to be your savior when you chose to confess it. But, in reality, know that God was there the whole time with His hand out, waiting for you to simply look up and place your hand in His—and you'd better believe that, once you reach out and grab His hand, He will never let go or give up on you.

Remember that the final hurdle is fear. So, are you feeling fear? Do you feel stupid asking for help out loud? These are simply the Devil's attempts to keep you in line with the fallen world rather than rising with Jesus. You have to fight through the demonic fear and say, "Jesus, I need you." It may sound easy, but it is one of the hardest things you will ever do. You can curse and swear, work 14-hour days, or even run a marathon with ease. But doing anything the first time *God* wants you to do it will be the hardest thing you ever do. However, once you step out and accomplish what God is asking you to do, peace and love will overflow in you—just as it is written in Colossians 2:7, which says, "overflowing with gratitude." Once you do or say whatever God is asking, you will immediately see how God's peace will replace all the fear that the Devil placed on you. You will see how incredibly good God is and automatically praise and give God thanks.

Here is a perfect example: Did you get saved just recently? If "Yes," praise the Lord! Even if you accepted Christ a long time ago, praise the Lord for the courage you had then to do so! Now for the perfect example. The Bible says that all that Jesus did, including dying on the cross so that we can receive the Holy Spirit, was done for one reason: to make you a new creation, one that now is a son or daughter of God himself. Now that you've accepted Jesus as Lord, the first gift He wants to give you is His Spirit and, with that, the gift of speaking in his language, which we call "speaking in tongues." Remember that you are His child, whom He loves more than anything, and that, if you ask, you shall receive. Try asking God for it. If you asked and it did not go well, or your mind took over again, that's OK. Remember that we are still learning and growing to trust in God through this whole process.

It does not matter what you have done in your past. God still wants you and loves you. Guess who has saved more people by their testimony of what Jesus has done than probably anyone else in history: The thief on the cross—someone so bad that the Roman state thought it better to kill him. He was being crucified next to Jesus. Even as he was dying, he was dealing with the same mental pain and struggle you do, and, at the very end, he looked at Jesus and simply said, "Jesus, remember me when you come into your kingdom." Jesus answered him and said, "Truly I say to you, today you shall be with Me in Paradise." The thief did no good *actions* for God; he simply believed. The world, and even other Christians, will tell you that, if you were really a Christian, you would not be doing this or that. They might tell you that, if you want God to bless you, you have to act a certain way, or give more, work harder, etc. Jesus made it clear: He is going to save you—not just when you die; that is settled since you made him Lord. But He also wants to bring heaven to you on this Earth.

If this is not happening, it is because you keep eating from the tree of death, the tree of the knowledge of good and evil. God's life is not in that. His life is in the Tree of life, and that life is in his son. So, to get that life of Heaven, you must hear God speak to you in every area of your life.

Here are some scriptures to meditate on that will help you understand that the Holy Spirit is with you today and that God is here to help you have the peace of heaven today on Earth.

John 14:16–17 *"16I will ask the Father, and He will give you another helper, that He may be with you forever; 17that is the Spirit of truth, whom the world cannot receive, because it does not see Him or know Him, but you know Him because He abides with you and will be in you."*

Galatians 5:22–25 *"22But the fruit of the Spirit is love, joy, peace, patience, kindness, goodness, faithfulness, 23gentleness, self-control; against such things there is no law. 24Now those who belong to Christ Jesus have crucified the flesh with its passions and desires. 25If we live by the Spirit, let us also walk by the Spirit."*

Matthew 6:10 *"Your kingdom come. Your will be done, on earth as it is in heaven."*

CHAPTER FOUR

GROWING
TO TRUST

Your inner voice has a sound

Remember, the cornerstone of Christianity and trusting in God is Jesus, who shows how much God loves you. Do not worry right now about understanding all of the ideas and details about Jesus and what He is or is not. As you grow with God and hear His voice more and more, God will reveal Himself to you in His time. Do not stress about trying to be exactly like Jesus, but rather focus on learning to trust God. Enjoy the process of growing in trust, and do not let anyone sway you.

God speaks to you non-stop, but it is your own mind and emotions that tend to shut Him out. If, by this point in reading this book, you have bought, dusted off, or even thought about getting a Bible, guess what? That was God. You may have thought it was your own thought, but it was God speaking to to your spirit, and you agreed with it. As you begin to spend more and more time reading the Bible, you may begin to see different verses or words that seem to jump off the page at you or cause you to really pause and take notice of them, as if an inner voice was saying, 'Hey, this is for you." When this happens, you may think, "Oh, this is not for me at all" or "This verse makes no sense." Some force is trying to get you to brush off the Bible verse, which is the word of God, and move on without understanding. This is the Devil's first line of defense in keeping you from hearing and knowing the truth about God. Those verses that seemingly jump off the page for you are one of the first ways God will speak to you and encourage you that He is right there with you. That verse jumped out at you because God *wanted* it to. This is the beginning of real faith.

However, faith is a two-way street. God will reach out to you, and then it is up to you to believe. This constant fight in your mind and spirit between God and the Devil continues even when reading the Bible. Will you believe what God is saying to you? Or will you believe what the Devil and the world have deemed logical to society? There are only two influencers, and you decide who you will listen to. The more often you choose to listen to what God is saying to you about your flesh, or worldly way of thinking, the less your flesh will influence you. In Christian terminology, this is called "killing the flesh." While the phrase "killing the flesh" may seem extreme, it is the only way to truly create an open channel between you and God, allowing Him to freely communicate with you. Once you can freely hear Him in all aspects of your life, all of the amazing promises that God has made to us will come to pass much easier.

> *"¹Therefore, since we have so great a cloud of witnesses surrounding us, let us also lay aside every encumbrance and the sin which so easily entangles us, and let us run with endurance the race that is set before us, ²fixing our eyes on Jesus, the author and perfecter of faith, who for the joy set before Him endured the cross, despising the shame, and has sat down at the right hand of the throne of God."*
> —HEBREWS 12:1–2

Jesus is the author and finisher of our faith. This means the responsibility of walking on the right path and trusting in God is not completely resting on you. Rather it is shared between you and Jesus. It is He who speaks to you, and, when you receive it, it becomes faith. The faith that comes from God is different from the world's definition of faith—"wishing for something to work out." Instead, it is the Godly spiritual faith that always works.

When the verse talks about how Jesus is the "finisher" of our faith, think back to the telescope on a pirate ship. God lets you see the end goal but it still takes time to get there. On the journey, storms arise, holes may form in the boat, and your crew may stage a mutiny, but by sticking to His words, the outside circumstances fall away. The destination you see through the telescope is your mark on this world, the destiny

God has planned for you. It will always come to pass if you don't stop believing. It is not a case of simply wanting it and claiming it, or picking a random scripture and saying, "I'm believing this verse for me." It has to be God Himself saying to you first: "This is what I want for you."

While the specifics of the journey of building trust in God differ from person to person, the general outline stays the same. First, God will speak to you where you are at, so that you can learn to trust the inner voice of His spirit. Then He will ask you to do something that seems simple, but something that takes you out of your comfort zone. As you listen and respond, as your faith and trust grow, He will start asking you to do bigger and bigger things. This is what "growing in God" means. It is not memorizing scripture after scripture or performing tasks that make other people deem you a "good Christian." Rather, it is growing in faith by God's spirit speaking to you. As you listen and respond, the things in this world that have been holding you back from experiencing peace and prosperity will fade into the background. God's voice becomes the center and focus of your life. The more of Him you have in your life, the more life you will have, because He is life and life everlasting.

Because hearing His voice is so essential to growing in faith, it is important to make sure you are hearing His voice clearly. The first step is to hear your own inner voice. In the past, many people who are learning to hear their own inner voice have told me that they "do not have an inner voice" or that they "cannot hear it." Rest assured that you do, in fact, have an inner voice and that it is amazingly easy to begin to hear it. Let's use you reading this book for example. As you read the words on the pages, do you hear yourself read the words in your mind? If you don't, and you think to yourself that you can't hear it yourself, how did you hear yourself think that? It is because this is the sound of your inner voice or thoughts; it is the voice of your spirit you are hearing. When your spirit wants something, it will affect your mind, which in turn makes your body react.

Be sure not to rush this step. Many people can't hear themselves at first. If you already can, then you are ahead of the game. However, if you cannot, set the book down for a moment and look around the room, describing things to yourself. Describe what you are seeing or imagining; look at things around the room, such as a picture, desk, lights, a couch, or a bed. Then move on to imagining things you would like to have, such as the new car you have been wanting for a while, or a brand-new little puppy. Describe them in detail to yourself—not out loud, but in your mind. Can you hear yourself? Try changing the volume of your thoughts. For example, look at the wall in front of you, and think to yourself, "This is a wall." Try whispering it to yourself; then try yelling it to yourself inside your mind. Can you feel the pressure in your head go from soft to hard as you change from whispering to yelling inside your mind? This is the real you, your spirit, the part of you that is eternal. Do not get discouraged by the sudden voices that may enter into your mind, such as "This is stupid. Why am I doing this?" This is, again, the Devil trying to keep you from realizing who you are with Christ and trying to keep you under his control. Making you think it is stupid, a waste of time, or worthless to keep trying are all strategies the Devil uses to keep you from growing in the freedom of God. By becoming aware of your inner voice, or spirit, and knowing that God talks to your spirit with His Spirit, suddenly verses like the one below begin to make more sense.

> *"²³ But an hour is coming, and now is, when the true worshipers will worship the Father in spirit and truth; for such people the Father seeks to be His worshipers. ²⁴ God is spirit, and those who worship Him* **must** *worship in spirit and truth."*
> —JOHN 4:23–24

So, to hear from God, you must hear Him with your spirit. But what is the truth that is referenced above when the verse says we will worship in "spirit and truth"? This is explained in John 17:17 when Jesus says, "Sanctify them in the truth; Your word is truth." Jesus is emphasizing that the truth is the Word of God, which includes everything that is written in the Bible and what God whispers to you each and every day.

Praise the Lord for Jesus and the fact that He has restored your spirit when you choose to believe in Him, so that He can now put His spirit inside of you to always be with you.

> *"¹⁷Therefore, if anyone is in Christ, he is a new creature; the old things passed away; behold new things have come. ¹⁸Now all these things are from God, who reconciles us to Himself*

through Christ and gave us the ministry of reconciliation,
[19] namely, that God was in Christ reconciling the world to
Himself, not counting their trespasses against them, and
He has committed to us the word of reconciliation."
—2 CORINTHIANS 5:17–19

Once you have accepted Christ, you are "born again" in the spirit and become a new creature, no longer bound by the sin of this world. You are free to follow God and His will for your life, knowing, without a doubt, that He will never leave you. Hebrews 13:5 reads, "Make sure that your character is free from the love of money, being content with what you have; for He Himself has said, 'I will never desert you, nor will I ever forsake you.'" It is one hundred percent assured that God will never leave or forsake you, however, you can forsake yourself. You destroy yourself when you refuse to hear God's voice and do not do what He is asking you. When you choose your fleshly will over God's will or let the fear Satan places inside of you take over and control your actions, you are forsaking yourself. This ruins the good and blessings that God is trying to give you. Romans 3:3–4 reads, "[3]What then? If some did not believe, their unbelief will not nullify their faithfulness of God, will it? [4]May it never be! Rather, let God be found true, though every man be found a liar, as it is written 'That you may be justified in your words, and prevail when you are judged.'"

Choosing to listen to God over what the world says is an everyday battle. In Genesis, it seems like Adam and Eve had to deal with the temptation only once, and failed, but we have to deal with it every single day with hundreds of choices. Adam and Eve walked with God in the Garden daily but still failed. We start off without any of God's spirit in us and have to win battle after battle in order to grow God's spirit within us as we continue to "kill the flesh." While it does not seem fair, understand that it is OK to make mistakes with this and that God continues to love you just as much as ever. As we continue to win battle after battle, we are able to free ourselves more to listen to God, making us stronger in Him and able to beat the Devil and his schemes more easily.

Remember that this battle is not a sprint—it is a marathon. Let God guide and teach you in it, and do not try to take off and do things on your own, because oftentimes you are not ready for it yet. Continually grow in God, hearing His voice and acting on it. With each win, your spirit realizes that the "real" world is actually the one in which you are walking with God Himself. Walking in God's world, in the true reality, is always good, and His spirit never leads you to trouble.

As I mentioned earlier, God's voice will sound like your own inner voice, just in a bit of a different pitch and tone. Think of it like a guitar: Both the top and bottom string make the note "E." While both strings are playing the same note, they do not sound exactly the same. This is similar to how hearing God's voice works. You and God are both E strings; while sounding different, both of you have the same style of speech. The more you recognize His voice, the more distinctive it becomes, and the easier you will recognize it. As you grow with God, the way He communicates with you will change, similar to how, as a baby grows, the parents begin to speak to their child differently.

We hear God speak to us all the time and do not recognize it. I remember the first time I heard God speak to me and knew in that moment that it was God. It was when I was on a mission trip in Fiji. At this point, I was already filled with the Spirit, and spoke in tongues, but I was angry because God would not speak to me. No one had discussed any of the things I mention in this book. For months, I would cry out day and night for God to talk to me. I would take walks at night, looking at the stars, saying things like, "Hey, God. Look at all these stars you created; look at this beautiful Earth. Are you telling me that you can create all this but not talk to me?" I went on and on, generally just ranting to God about wanting to hear Him. This went on until one night, I was on my walk, and, while overlooking some hills by myself, I noticed that I was getting answers in response to my questioning thoughts. So, I asked a few more questions, and immediately answers came back. I asked, "Is this God?" and immediately heard back, "Yes, it is." In all honesty, I freaked out at this point. My next immediate thought was, "I thought God could not talk to me like this." Instead of answering, God asked back, "Why not?" That's when I realized how cool God is. Think about it: He made you, so He knows how best to talk to you. For the rest of the night, I sat there with God and enjoyed small talking with Him. After a while, I asked Him who I was going to marry, and imme-diately, what felt like a wall between God and me came up. This "wall" I now recognize as spiritual fear or anxiousness.

This is an important detail. Even though we are saved and born again so that God's spirit can live in us, we still have to continually renew our Earthly and anxious mind in Him. This "wall" that came up between God and me when I was speaking to Him was a result of being anxious over the answer. This has happened often to me since that moment. When our mind is full of anxiety, stress, or fear over what God's answer may be, our flesh cuts off the connection between God's voice and us. This is why, in Philippians 4:6–7, Jesus explains, "⁶Be anxious for nothing, but in everything by prayer and supplication with thanksgiving let your requests be made known to God. ⁷And the peace of God, which surpasses all comprehension, will guard your hearts and your minds in Christ Jesus." Notice how in this verse, it specifies "in Christ Jesus"? This happens all over the New Testament, but what exactly does it mean? Think about it like this: What was inside of Jesus Christ? It was the Holy Spirit of God, the same Spirit living inside of you today once you accept Christ. This is why Jesus came to sacrifice Himself and take away the sins of the world, so that He could give His Spirit to the world. This is also why, all throughout the New Testament, Jesus repeatedly says *those who believe "in" me.* It is not just believing that Jesus was a real person, but rather believing in the fact that He was the son of God, and that the same spirit of God that lived in Him now lives in you and me.

So, if you begin to hear and speak with God and feel this wall come up, what do you do? Remember that the wall appeared in the first place because you were wanting or expecting a certain answer from God and/or were fearful of what the answer may be. It is always easier when you are listening to, and being led by, God's spirit speaking to you. When you turn this around and start speaking to God, demanding what you need and how soon it must be done, it becomes hard to hear God's will for you in the situation. When this happens, it becomes extremely easy to misunderstand what the Lord wants to say to you, resulting in you falling under outside influences and the temptation of the world, which are not from the Lord. You become so reliant on your own understanding of the world that you fail to see the bigger plan God has for you. You end up relying on your worldly knowledge to "fix" the situation with what you believe needs to be done. Relying on your worldly knowledge will get you into trouble every single time. You have to hear from God on everything, while not demanding an answer or solution right away. It is for this reason that King David always makes statements such as in Psalms 27:14, "Wait for the Lord; Be strong and let your heart take courage; Yes, wait for the Lord." Or Psalms 62:5: "My soul, wait in silence for God only, for my hope is from Him."

Most people reach out to God only when they are stressed and need help immediately. God understands this, but the problem that comes from doing this is that, when we are under extreme stress, it is close to impossible to hear Him clearly. This is why, written above in Psalms 62:5, King David tells himself to calm down and wait in silence. King David is actually telling his anxious self and spirit to calm down and wait for God in the stillness of his own heart and mind rather than demanding immediate answers and then acting on his own worldly knowledge when he does not get them. Quieting your mind and spirit is much easier said than done, which is why it is important to set aside time each day to come before God, listen to Him, and then go on with the day based on what you have heard. Trust me—this way works much easier than going out each day, running into trouble, and then playing catch-up on your stress while begging God for help. We all believe that God wants us happy and healthy, but then we cannot understand why God does not hear or answer our prayers. The main reason is that *prayer means calming down and listening to God*, not demanding Him to do things and telling Him exactly when to do so.

If you are praying and feel a wall come up, turning your peaceful conversation with God into scattered thoughts about the many stressful, and often unnecessary, "What if?" scenarios, remember to calm down and quiet your mind and spirit. Again, this is easier said than done, but there are several steps you can go through to help quiet your spirit and find yourself resting once again in God's presence. First, tell yourself, out loud or in your mind, to calm down. Second, once calm, do not immediately think back to the subject that caused turmoil in your mind in the first place. Instead, talk to God about something else. After a while, your mind and emotions will be under control, and the Spirit of God will start talking to you about an easier subject. You may still feel a small portion of the wall standing, but as you rest more into God's presence, it will completely fade away.

As you build confidence again and realize that you are communicating freely with God, oftentimes He will suddenly give you the answer to whatever was causing turmoil for you in the first place. Remember that God is our teacher, and, just as teachers in school will teach the same material several different ways, so does God. He will come from different angles, allowing you to learn more easily from Him. Think of it like this: A wall comes up with you on one side of it and God on the other. As you are staring at this wall, or maybe even hitting it, trying to force it to come down, God comes around the other side of the wall and slowly starts speaking to you. As you begin to focus more on Him than on the wall, the wall begins to fall. This will happen again and again to you on your walk with God. It is simply who we are as children of God, learning more each day to trust in Him and to kill the doubts and lies that the Devil has put into our hearts and minds.

It is OK for the wall to come up sometimes or for you to make mistakes. This is how we all grow. Your mind and spirit are growing in the knowledge of hearing and believing in God. God is patient and understands you perfectly. So, as frustrating as it may be, stick with the process when you become anxious, calming yourself down and letting Him talk about other things with you until He gives you His will for the stressful subject. When this happens, oftentimes, we stress out again and then calm back down, in a cycle, until we are at peace with God once again. This process builds in our mind and spirit the belief that we are, indeed, hearing correctly from God and can fully trust Him. It also builds the confidence in us to act on what God is saying to us, because we have heard it in so many different ways that we can be completely sure that it is from the Lord. Then, when it comes to pass, we are filled with joy and excitement from the confirmation once again that we are hearing from God Himself. As this process continues, we are able to handle bigger and bigger things that He asks us to do.

Do not be discouraged by this process. Even King David grew to trust God in this same way. David did not just walk up to Goliath one day out of the blue with ease. Instead, he had been working for years, learning to trust God while tending his father's sheep out in the fields. Then, when it came time for him to step up to the next level and continue to his destiny, defeating the giant Goliath, David was able to look back and see how God had brought him through the past events in his life for this moment. Then David recognizes that he is under the protection of God. In 1 Samuel 17:37, it says, "And David said, 'The Lord who delivered me from the paw of the lion and from the paw of the bear, He will deliver me from the hand of this Philistine."

Think back to the story of when I knew I'd heard God for the first time. After I asked about my future wife, became anxious about the answer, and felt the wall come up, God came around the wall to me, and we slowly began to small talk once again. This time I did not ask Him about who I was going to marry, instead keeping the conversation safe and easy. We continued chatting until God said something, and I questioned whether it was true or not. God told me to look for the truth in the Bible, even giving me the book, chapter, and verse. Immediately, doubt from the enemy entered my mind, along with fear. What if it was not there? What if this means that I am not actually hearing from God? It took a while for me to overcome this fear and actually look in the Bible, and there it was! I was relieved and ecstatic. In my joy, God spoke to me again, giving me another book, chapter, and verse to look for. Immediately those same fears came back. I had just been overwhelmed with joy from hearing God, and as soon as I had to trust that what I'd heard was true, once again I was fearful, until I again built up the nerve to look—and there it was!

Almost every time God asks you to do or say something, this same process will happen to you. Your flesh, or mind and emotions, do not want to give up any ground that the Devil has claimed in you. Once I found that the second verse God gave me was there, just as He'd said it would be, the joy was immediately back. God and I small talked a little bit more, and He gave me another verse. I looked it up, and it was not there. I felt so defeated. I walked back to the group who were on the mission trip with me and told them the story, about how I thought I'd heard from the Lord but the scripture He gave me was not there. The leader asked what scripture I had heard. I said, "Jeremiah 3:33, which does not exist." She then suggested, "God probably said Jeremiah 33:3." I looked up Jeremiah 33:3—and there it was: The exact thing that God and I were talking about when I thought I'd heard the verse wrong! Jeremiah 33:3 says, "Call to Me and I will answer you, and I will tell you great and mighty things, which you do not know." I was amazed.

As exciting as my story is, it is important to remember that we are continually growing in the Lord and, as a result, can "miss" what He is saying to us. Just because I misheard God speak a specific verse to me does not mean that I did not hear God at all. Remember that you and I have a lot of ground to cover and take back from the enemy in our mind and spirit. Do not worry about others thinking poorly of you if you "miss" it or mishear from God. Instead, celebrate, because you are hearing Him in the first place! Since then, I have "missed" it over and over. God will speak to us, and as soon as we have the basis of what He is saying to us, we take that simple thought and run with it, continuing with our own knowledge and strength. Eventually, we mess it up and have to go back to God. But as you continue to grow in Him and gain a deeper understanding of how perfect God is in all of His ways, the easier it becomes to fully trust in Him and His plans alone. Then, if you mishear or make a mistake, it is easier to go back to God, asking where you missed it, versus blaming God for it not working out. Either way, He always lovingly shows us where the mistake happened, and we can move on. Everything God tells you to do is always in your best interest.

CHAPTER FIVE

STRENGTH IN PATIENCE

You will know when you get off course

Now that you have a deeper understanding of what hearing God's voice is like, and how it starts as a small, gentle whisper that matches your own form of speech, it is time to learn how God speaks to us when we are about to do something that will be bad for us. When we go to do something extremely detrimental to our well-being, that still, small voice can turn into a voice that is intense and hard to ignore. Think about when you were growing up and were with your family. Everything could be going fine, but as soon as you decided to step out onto a busy street, one of your parents quickly yelled at you to stop. The yell from your parent broke through all of the current thoughts you had in your mind to cross the street and made you stop what you were doing immediately. It is the same with God's voice trying to stop you from doing something harmful to yourself.

Take a moment and think of a time that someone has done this for you, or you have done this for a loved one, to keep them from danger. Keep in mind, though, that God is love, and do not compare Him telling you to stop to a human yelling at you with the intent to control you. That is what the Devil does. The Devil pushes you, and constantly presses your spirit and mind to do something that, in your heart and spirit, you know you should not. When this happens, God, being love, jumps up and yells, "Stop!" in your spirit when you are in imminent danger.

I understand—no one wants a friend or loved one who is always telling them what to do or how to act and live every single day. Our human nature applies this to God as well. Once we learn that God is real and that we are able to hear His voice, many people want to turn off everything that God created them to be. Instead, we think that we need to be a robot that cannot move or decide anything without hearing the exact word from Him, but this is not what God intended. Once you begin hearing God, having conversations with Him, and learning about who He is, you reach a point where you do not receive directions for every little thing, and you begin to get nervous that maybe God has left you or that you can no longer hear Him. It was the same for me. After I realized I could hear God, I would ask things like "Which shirt should I wear today?" or "What cereal should I have for breakfast?" on and on for every single detail of my day. Then all of a sudden, I would not get an answer. Internal stress would build up as I began to think that I'd done something wrong or that God had left me. The Devil, being one to take advantage of every weakness we have, would be right there, adding more fear and doubt. Eventually, the Lord would break through the cloud of stress and fear I had created around myself and calm me down, explaining that He wants a relationship with me, not a dictatorship. He explained that I was at the point in my relationship with Him that I did not need to be spoon fed and held like a baby any longer, needing help with every single thing in life. Instead, I now had enough of God's thoughts and understanding in me to be able to take some steps on my own.

As we begin to grow with God, our relationship with Him changes from that of a child into that of an adult. When this happens, God is able to trust us with bigger and bigger things for us to accomplish here on Earth. An example of this is God asking me to write this book. To be honest, it took me a while to believe that He was actually asking me to write a book about Him. But as always, He showed me over and over in the Bible different examples of people listening to His instruction, even though it made no sense at the time, and, as a result of listening and obeying, they were blessed. I took comfort in the fact that, when the people in the Bible got off course, God was right there to encourage them and show them the right direction. God did not micromanage them or say things like, "Put your left foot here, and your right foot there." Once you have learned to clearly hear God, you are able to take more and more steps on your own, similar to learning how to walk, where your parents support you until you can walk on your own. God loves seeing you learn to walk with Him on your own. Remember, He is trying to grow you into a "child of God," not a slave or robot. Romans 8:15 reads, "For you have not received a spirit of slavery leading to fear again, but you have received a spirit of adoption as sons by which we cry out, 'Abba! Father!'" Remember this when you begin to feel like God is not there. This means that you are starting to grow up spiritually, believing in what God has taught you.

This is also around the time in your walk with God that He begins to teach you spiritual patience. When you do not hear Him on every little thing, it is easy to get frustrated. You love God, but without receiving constant positive reinforcement from Him, anxiety starts to creep in. When in this stage, your old worldly mind can wreak havoc on you, and the next thing you know, you start to go somewhere or do something that you know in your spirit is wrong. That feeling in your spirit is the Holy Spirit nudging you. When we continue down the path that is not right, even though the Holy Spirit lives inside of us and we can hear God's voice, we are still full of what we have learned from the Devil and the world before we accepted God. This is why God teaches us how to overcome this fleshly influence over our lives. But as we continue down a path to knowingly do something wrong, right at the moment that our flesh or mind seems like it is physically pushing us to step out of the will of God, the Holy Spirit will directly, in an incredibly strong inner, and sometimes an almost physically audible voice, tell us to "STOP." This voice can be so strong that we hear Him in our bones. Because of our fallen nature, even with God calling to us in this way, we still make mistakes, pushing through God's warning to commit whatever we were about to do. As soon as that happens, the Devil immediately jumps onto you, beating you with words, telling you that you can never go back to God after what you have done, or that God will never accept you again because you went against Him, or that God is extremely angry with you.

Do not let these thoughts settle in your spirit! Remember that God loves you yesterday, today, and tomorrow, the exact same amount, and that nothing you do, or do not do, will make God love you any less. Rather than being angry at you, God mourns for you, knowing the pain that stepping outside of His will causes. God eagerly awaits the moment that you come running back to Him. In that moment, He can restore and love on you, telling you that He forgives you and giving you endless opportunities to try again. One of the best ways to learn how to keep your old self from ruling is to have that deep-set understanding that God loves you with everything He has, and that God has already defeated every single sin, ever, in Christ Jesus. Once you have this deep understanding, it becomes much easier to immediately come back to God after messing up, knowing you failed, but also knowing that God loves you, immediately forgives you, and is excited to help you learn, improve, and try again.

Know that, through Jesus Christ, God has defeated every sin. This mean *all* sins—past, present, and future. You may think to yourself, "You don't understand. Some of the things I have done cannot be forgiven" or "If you only knew the shameful things I have done, you would not be telling me this." Guess what? Since the fall of Adam and Eve, there have been no new sins on this Earth. Everyone struggles with almost the exact same things, and the Devil tries to keep you chained to them through shame or guilt. There is no shame or guilt in God, and He would never lay these feelings onto you. Praise the Lord that God has broken those chains for us through Jesus Christ! Know that, whether it's shame from porn addiction, past hookups, drunkenness, hate, drugs, or really anything that you feel you have to keep hidden in the dark, God knows about it, fully forgives you, and still loves you more than you will ever know.

The Devil wants you to think and behave like you are a failure for as long as he can. He will try to keep you dwelling on the sins you have committed and thinking that you have to do something yourself before God will be pleased with you and accept you. The is one of the biggest lies of the Devil. Remember that God has forgiven all of your sins, even the ones you will commit in the future. So, as quickly as you can, run back to the Spirit of the Lord, which never left you and still lives inside of you, and repent. Repenting does not mean what the world has made it seem like—where you grovel on your hands and knees, begging for forgiveness. Repenting to God is as simple as telling God "You were right, I was wrong, and I'm sorry" and then going right back to growing in Him.

It can be strange and intimidating when you are used to spending time with God, with Him speaking to you in a gentle voice, and then, suddenly, when you go off course, that gentle voice switches to one that makes you stop in your tracks, feeling almost sick inside. Praise the Lord for this! Not only does it reaffirm that God is always with you, but it mirrors scripture. Proverbs 3:12 reads, "For whom the Lord loves He corrects, even as a father corrects the son in whom he delights." Like I said before, it is similar to when you are corrected by a parent when you are about to do something wrong. They start off telling you gently that you should not be doing that, but when it comes to the point where you make the decision to do it anyway, getting into harm's way, they sternly tell you to stop. This is the same way God the Father corrects us. Personally, this took me decades to fully understand. Every day, I would be working and asking God again and again, "What now? What's next?" I never got another answer except, "You are fine." However, when I would begin to go astray, after my fleshly mind would convince me that these worldly things would bring me joy, right before I would step past the point of no return, the Holy Spirit would instantly be there, telling me to stop.

While this struggle—our spirit and flesh battling each other—continues, God is great and is right there next to us during it. Along with telling you to stop right before the point of no return, God is good and will help you directly in the decision points leading up to this. There are many inner battles that lead up to the final point of no return. Often people continue down the wrong path because they don't want to let their friends down or be embarrassed. They may think, "I *have* to continue, because I made plans with my friends, and I don't want them to think that I'm not a person of my word" or

"Well, there are certainly worse things that I could be doing." These thoughts enter your mind and begin to spiral until you give into them. This is the Devil trying to push you along the wrong path, toward destruction.

Remember that God is always with you and that, when you find yourself facing these decision points, God *will* provide a way for you to escape if you ask Him, saving your reputation and you in the process. It works every time because God is great and fulfills every promise He has made to you. 1 Corinthians 10:13 reads, "No temptation has overtaken you but such as is common to man; and God is faithful, who will not allow you to be tempted beyond what you are able, but with the temptation will provide the way of escape also, so that you will endure it." It is amazing how loving God is to provide a way out for us when it seems like all the pressure of the world is practically *forcing* us to step away from Him. While it sounds simple, just having to ask for it, it can be challenging at first, because it is the first step in a process of growing. You have to put God's will above your own and trust Him completely, doing what God says to do in order to get out of the situation. This can be scary the first few times, because it's new to you; however, you should never forget that God is working in you for your good.

I struggled with this at first, as well. I used to say, "God, I need you to make this work. It is *my* face that people see. Please don't let me be embarrassed." This is all a part of the growing process in learning that God is faithful, keeps all of His promises and covenants, and loves all those who keep His commandments. But most of all, you must realize that God is completely *for* you and is never *against* you. The more you continue to believe in the voice of God inside of you, the more you will be able to get out of these seemingly impossible situations without embarrassment. When I speak of God loving all those who keep His commandments, I don't mean the Old Testament Ten Commandments or all of the many other rules that God gave His people throughout the Old Testament. The Devil has used all of those rules to twist the minds of Christians into believing that they have to perfectly follow all of those rules in order to earn God's favor. This is not to say that the whole of the Old Testament is no longer important—it is still the Word of God. If you let the Holy Spirit guide you when reading through it, He will reveal much to you about what exactly is meant by the words and rules. However, this is exactly why God sent Jesus to the Earth—so that now we are found guiltless before God as long as we believe in Him. Now, after Jesus cleansed us of our sins, God's commandments are those that He speaks to you through His spirit, which lives inside of you. Now you can live with a God who *personally* knows you and guides you daily to be victorious in this life. The path God has given you is unique to you personally; don't try to model it after anyone in the past or present. Instead, simply listen to God, and let His protection and peace surround you. Feel secure in the fact that the God Who created everything is always right there with you, every single day.

So, what do you do when you are unsure of what exactly He wants you to do? You may be seeking, asking, praying, and reading His word but not getting a clear answer. First, remember that you need to put your mind and spirit to rest, as we talked about earlier. Oftentimes, when facing a big decision, we will stress ourselves so much over needing answers that it's hard to hear God. Everything may seem fine, but, when speaking with God, you start to push for specifics on subjects that are important to you, and it seems like He will not give you an answer. You say to yourself, "I can hear God clearly on everything else. Why can't I hear Him on this?"

One of the main reasons is that the issue is especially important to you, resulting in your mind and body becoming anxious and stressed over it. The stress in your mind is keeping your spirit from hearing His spirit clearly. We are born again when we accept Christ, but even then—filled with the Holy Spirit—our mind and body are still from this world, which is of a fallen nature. This means that God has to get through our worldly mind and into our renewed spirit in order for us to hear Him clearly and easily. It is similar to how, when we are extremely stressed, it becomes hard for us to think clearly. God understands this and has made a way for us to still hear him, even when we ourselves are unable to clearly think.

Let's take Luke, the writer of the book of Luke, as an example. He starts off the book with these verses:

"¹In as much as many have undertaken to compile an account of the things accomplished among us, ²just as they were handed down to us by those who from the beginning were eyewitnesses and servants of the word,

³it seemed fitting for me as well, having investigated everything carefully from the beginning, to write it out for you in consecutive order, most excellent Theophilus; ⁴so that you may know the exact truth about the things you have been taught."

—LUKE 1:1–4

These verses from the beginning of the book of Luke are talking about the attempt to record and compile all of the acts of Jesus and the Holy Spirit while Jesus was here on Earth. In verse 3, take notice of the word "seemed." The author of this book, Luke, was a very well-educated man. Luke was a doctor, but he was also a spirit-filled man, who walked with Jesus and did the best he could each day to hear from God and walk by the Holy Spirit leading him. But you can see here in these opening verses that Luke struggled to write the book. He admits that others had already written the accounts of Christ; he seems to be wondering to himself why God would also want him to write an additional account. If Luke was a doctor, then reasonings such as being "too busy" were going through his mind, also. The battle that we spoke of earlier was real inside of him, with the Devil telling him the same things that you have probably heard before: "I'm not good enough for this." "I have no time." "I am a doctor, not a writer." "I will leave it to the writers to do it better themselves." However, in the middle of all of this, God reminded him that he had investigated everything carefully for himself. Luke came to realize that, at the time when he was investigating, it was from God's prompting.

Even with all of Luke's preparation in knowing the full life and story of Christ, when God asked Luke to write a book, he became extremely stressed about it. Luckily, Luke knew the voice of the Lord well enough to know that it was, indeed, God prompting him to write. Luke deeply understood that God is love and that God was with and in him. So, even though there were already many books on the life of Christ, Luke chose to listen to God and write one himself. As a result, we have the book of Luke in the Bible today. While not being able to hear God completely clearly on the matter, Luke, having established a relationship with God before this moment, did what "seemed fitting" in writing the book. He knew that, with God's help, he would break through the stress of his mind and that God was big enough to warn him if he were going in the wrong direction.

It is the same for you. When it seems like the stress of the universe is pressing down on you, and you cannot clearly hear exactly what God wants you to do, do what seems fitting. After you establish a relationship with God as a base, more and more of God's character rubs off on you as you grow and spend more time with Him. Because of this, oftentimes what "seems fitting" or correct is actually the correct way to go. Remember and trust in the fact that, if you start to head in the wrong direction, the Lord will let you know. But up until that point, if your heart is not convicting you, keep moving in the direction that seems clear to you until the internal storm of stress stops, at which point you will be able to clearly hear God on the situation.

It is not our job to be perfect every step of the way. It is simply our job to do the best we can with the words that the Spirit of God has spoken to us, so that, one day, when we are standing in front of God, we can say with confidence that we did the best we could with the knowledge that we had.

When faced with challenging moments, look back on your life and everything that you have been learning from God all along. There is a good chance that you are more prepared for it than you first believed, whether you knew it was God guiding you through different experiences or not. Your life experiences are different from anyone else's in this world, and because of that, God is able to use you in a way different from the way he might use anyone else in this world. Even though, in the past, you made decisions on your own, without first listening to God's voice on the matter, He has been training you all along. Don't worry about where God is leading you, because you can be sure that you will be well prepared before you get there. Along the way, simply walk in the direction He gives you, and when you feel like you cannot hear Him, just continue to walk in the same direction in which you *did* hear him. You will find His peace waiting for you there.

Now that we know how to continue in the direction God wants us to walk, even when we cannot clearly hear Him, we need to get to the root of the problem—why the stress causes us to become anxious and worried in this world. What is causing all of this stress that seemingly comes with walking in the direction that God gives you? The simple answer is the same for every single human who has walked on this Earth: It is the love and deceitfulness of money, which happens to also be the root of sin. When you get to the core of the fear and stress that seem to come with following God's plan for your life, it is often because you think that you will not be fully provided for—that you will run out of or not have enough money. Our minds are naturally filled with what the world has taught us about making and saving money, and oftentimes that worldly thinking will not line up with God's thinking. The Devil will often give you thoughts such as, "How can I make a living doing this? What will my friends think of my giving up this opportunity? What will my family think? Maybe I should wait to do this until I have saved up some more and learned more about it. Maybe I should wait until I get some confirmation from something or someone." Thoughts like these will run through your mind, flooding you with the decision-making logic based on the world's knowledge. This results in your mind becoming stressed and confused, paralyzing you from knowing God's will in your life.

Do not get down on yourself when this happens, because the same thing will happen to everyone at some point in their walk with Christ. When you reach this point, celebrate! It is known as a trial; hearing how others have overcome trials and then overcoming them yourself will bring you joy. While hearing how someone faced, and overcame, a trial is much less stressful than facing one yourself; rest assured that the joy that comes from overcoming is more than worth the struggle.

"²Consider it all a joy, my brethren, when you encounter various trials, ³knowing that the testing of your faith produces endurance. ⁴And let endurance have its perfect result, so that you may be perfect and complete, lacking in nothing."

—JAMES 1:2–4

After experiencing a few trials, it will almost become a fun challenge to you. You become stronger realizing that the Spirit of God that speaks inside of you always wins against the lies that the world has taught you. You become stronger and surer of God and of who you are as a son or daughter of God. You are no longer someone who thinks of yourself as a regular person; rather, you begin to realize exactly who you are in God. You are a son or daughter of God, the God who created everything we know of and more, His child who talks and works with Him daily, knowing that you can accomplish everything that He asks you to do. You begin to deeply realize just how incredibly proud God is of you.

God is leading you into His kingdom here in this life. You don't have to wait until the day you die to enter God's Kingdom. When you walk with His spirit, you are walking in the kingdom today. Let this knowledge settle deep into your spirit, that you are walking in the kingdom of God here on Earth, today. Stepping out with God can be scary, because the worldly knowledge will go against you from almost every direction, but remember that God is above all of that. So, when He asks you to do something, rest assured that it will come to pass as long as you stay with God. These trials mentioned above happen inside of you, inside of your mind. As much as you can look at the circumstances to justify your fears, know that it is not the circumstances that matter—it's God. Instead of focusing on the circumstances causing the trial, focus on God. It was the same for Peter, when he stepped out of the boat during a storm to walk on the water to Jesus. As soon as he looked at the big waves surrounding him, which is similar to you looking at the stressful circumstances surrounding you, he began to sink. Only after Peter refocused on Jesus, calling out to Him, and focusing only on Him, was he able to stand above the waves once again, and the stormed calmed. It is the same for you. Focus on God and your trust in him rather than on the waves surrounding you. Then you will be able to walk on calm waters to where God is leading you.

Think of all of the trials you are currently facing, and try saying out loud, with as much joy as you can, "God, I thank you for watching over me and loving me. I thank you for Your Spirit, who is guiding me toward this new journey. It makes the Devil so afraid that he is trying to stop me with every thought of fear that he can imagine. Lord, I know you are good and that you love me. I can see how much you have helped and guided me in the past, and I am going to go forward with what I believe seems right in this decision before me." Hebrews 11:1 reads, "Now faith is the assurance of things hoped for, the conviction of things not seen." Read through the rest of Hebrews 11, and look at all of the great names of the people in the Bible who had to deal with the same struggles you are facing right now. This is your time. This is the age you were created for. This life is where you are able to have the same faith, if not more, than those listed in Hebrews 11, and if you continue your walk with God each day, you will.

CHAPTER SIX

HOPE

You can miss it by trusting in yourself

*"So these three things continue forever: Faith, hope,
and love. And the greatest of these is love."*
—1 CORINTHIANS 13:13

This well-known scripture addresses faith, hope, and love.
The ideas in this book are also grouped in the same way,
except the Lord put it into my heart to do so in reverse, cov-
ering love, hope, and then faith. Without fully understanding
how much God loves you, it is hard to understand spiritual
faith and hope. The greatest of these three things is love, and,
therefore, it was taught first. Once love is the cornerstone of
your relationship with God, of trusting in Him, and of having
faith that He will always be there for you, then hope can begin
to form in your spirit.

It is important to truly know what "hope" means. The
English word "hope" is a combination of two Greek words
which mean: expectation, hope, trust, confidence, properly,

expectation of what is sure or certain, to expect, trust, actively waiting for God's fulfillment about faith He has in-birthed through the power of His love (Strong's Numbers 1679 & 1680). This differs greatly from today's common use of the word "hope," which instead can often mean, "I guess," "You never know," or "It may or may not happen." Rest assured, however, that God is real, and hearing His voice is why He sent Jesus to take away the sins of the world and allow the Holy Spirit to enter us. Isaiah 55:6–12 says, "⁶Seek the Lord while He may be found; call upon Him while He is near. ⁷Let the wicked forsake his way and the unrighteous man his thoughts; and let him return to the Lord, and He will have compassion on him, and to our God, for He will abundantly pardon. ⁸'For My thoughts are not your thoughts, nor are your ways My ways,' declares the Lord. ⁹'For as the heavens are higher than the earth, so are My ways higher than your ways and My thoughts than your thoughts. ¹⁰For as the rain and the snow come down from heaven, and do not return there without watering the earth and making it bear and sprout, and furnishing seed to the sower and bread to the eater; ¹¹So will My word be which goes forth from My mouth; it will not return to Me empty, without accomplishing what I desire, and without succeeding in the matter for which I sent it. ¹²For you will go out with joy and be led forth with peace; the mountains and the hills will break forth into shouts of joy before you, and all the trees of the field will clap their hands.'"

God speaks to you. He speaks inside of you, differently from the way your own thoughts sound. While it sounds like it is from inside of you, it almost feels like it is coming from a different part of you, from your spirit. This is what the Bible means when it speaks of the "heart" of you—it is the real you. When God speaks something to you, it is one hundred percent guaranteed to happen if you follow His instruction to make it so. You must believe that God is going to follow through with His word in and through you. This is spiritual hope, and God longs to show you that He stands behind what He says. When He speaks to you, it will come to pass. God values His word as much as His name. Psalms 138:2 reads, "I will bow down facing your holy Temple, and I will thank you for your love and loyalty. You have made your name and your word greater than anything" (New Century Version). Do not be afraid that, when you start hearing God, He will ask you to do something beyond what is possible for you. Rather He will give you glimpses into how good the path He is leading you down is, all while slowly walking you toward your goal, giving you guidance and help along the way. He desires for you to build trust in yourself, trust that you are hearing from Him, and trust in Him before beginning to challenge you. It is similar to a newborn child. We naturally have more patience with them than with a 12-year-old, and we also celebrate more with each milestone for a newborn, for example, first steps or their first words in life. As the child grows, we begin to expect more and more of them. It is the same with God. He starts off small and then adds expectations as you gain confidence and skill. All of this is done in His love for you and His faithfulness to His word and to you.

God begins to challenge you as you grow in the confidence that you are hearing Him clearly, because you are now walking by the direction of the Spirit of God, which, as we discussed earlier, will always seem to contrast the way you used to make decisions and the way the world teaches you to think. Every time God asks you to do something, your fleshly mind and emotions will try to go against it, saying it is not logical. Your mind will begin grabbing everything it can from your memory to tell you why it cannot be done or how it will be embarrassing. However, don't worry, because the more you grow in God, the easier it will be to become victorious over your own flesh until the point where you no longer doubt His spirit. Everyone goes through this same process; this is how we are as humans learning to grow in the knowledge of the new life God is guiding us to live in. This is also what God means when it says in the Bible that we have to take His kingdom by force. You have to muster up the courage and strength to say to your own mind, "Be quiet. Emotions, calm down. I know that God is for me." Instead of filling your mind with doubt, choose to remember how God has spoken to you previously and how it came to pass. A good way to do this is to play the game "Remember When." It is a simple game, in which you just say to yourself, out loud, all that God has done for you. You simply say, "God, I remember when you helped me out in this situation" or "God, I remember when you helped me out of that sticky situation." Go into detail in this game, and you will be amazed at how many things you can remember that God has done for you.

Doing this will give you the courage to do whatever God is asking of you. When you gather the courage to step out and act on what He is telling you, it is called works of "faith." If you step out in faith and you fail, it's easy to get discouraged, but don't. Let's examine a few reasons why this might have happened. One of the main reasons I see is when someone receives a word from the Lord, and, without listening to instructions on how to accomplish it, they take the word and then rely on their own worldly knowledge to make it happen. They no longer rely on God to make His word come to pass, but rather place that stress and burden on themselves. When this happens, and they fail, they become stressed and begin to doubt if they ever heard God's voice; they begin to complain how God let them down. This is a common mistake for every new Christian to make, because we are still learning how to follow God's voice. Instead of wallowing in self-pity for weeks or months, make it a point to get over this hurdle as quickly as possible and ask God to show you where you missed it. Just get alone with God and start small talking to Him again, then when you are back in fellowship with Him, He will guide you in the right direction. He will show you where you missed it, and you will grow closer to Him through this process.

It is so easy to make this mistake because we have to have patience, and that is hard to have when we see the visions of grandeur from following God's word. We all want to be like King David, killing giants in the name of the Lord and getting the fame and honor for it. In fact, even Joshua made this same mistake. Even though Joshua had won many battles over the years, he always asked God for the strategy in each one. However, one day when there was a small army to battle, Joshua believed he could do it without God's instructions, and, as a result, he lost the battle. Right after the battle, Joshua repented and went back to God, asking for His wisdom in the next battle. We can do the same; don't get down on yourself. The Devil loves to make us think that we are a failure and hold no value, but, as we have discussed, this is not true! Instead we have the ability to go straight back to God and gain wisdom and knowledge through Him to enable us to easily win the next battle.

Another reason we can miss what God is really saying to us, causing His word not to come to pass, is by pushing God into a timetable. When we hear God's word, and ask God for a specific date and time, and then get no answer, we will press and press until we believe we have heard an exact date and time from Him. I have never heard of God giving someone an exact date or time, but He will sometimes give us a season in which what He speaks will happen. The process to get back on the right road with God is the same as above—simply go to God, humble yourself, and ask for guidance in what the next step is.

I have made the mistake of pushing God into a timetable many times as well. I used to own a piece of property that the Lord wanted me to sell. At the time, I was in the mission field and was set to return in a couple of months. I called a realtor while overseas and asked them to put it on the market. I was so proud that I did what God had asked, and I fully believed that it would happen—it was almost like the property had already been sold! All because I already had God's word on it. A month went by, and I still did not have a single offer. I began to stress and tell God that I needed it sold now. In reality, I did not truly need it to be sold. I simply did not want to have to deal with it when I came home. I pushed and pushed God until I felt like the Lord told me it would be sold before I landed in Los Angeles, which is where I lived at the time. Even on the flight home, I fully believed it would be sold before the wheels touched down and that the people picking me up from the airport would tell me it had sold. But that did not happen, and I was crushed. I put all the blame on God for several days. Eventually, however, I repented and asked God to help me understand where I had missed it. To be honest, at this time I still did not believe that I had messed up anywhere. With all the stress and anxiety still in my mind from the property not selling, I felt in my heart like I should call the man who had bought the last property I sold, to see if he might be interested. Instantly, I was filled with fear over doing this, not wanting to call, only for to him reject me. But the same thought kept coming up in my spirit. I finally understood that it was the Lord speaking to me. I found the man's number and called, and it turned out he was interested and even paid cash for the property. This was God's first lesson in teaching me to not pressure Him for an exact time on things He speaks to me. However, even to this day, I find myself falling into this same trap. I have to take a step back and remember those moments when it worked out better when, instead of pressuring God, I simply trusted in Him to make it happen on His timeline, not mine.

Trust me when I say that you did hear God's voice on something, even if it did not come to pass. Take a moment to go back to God and ask where you missed it. We have to continue to have faith in God and to place our Hope, our absolute trust, in Him. Hope is being absolutely sure that what God has said to you will become visible in this world. Even if you do not physically see it yet, rest assured that it is happening. Jesus says a similar thing in Luke 17:20–21: "²⁰Some of the Pharisees asked Jesus, 'When will the kingdom of God come?' Jesus answered, 'God's kingdom is coming, but not in a way that you will be able to see with your eyes. ²¹People will not say, 'Look, here it is!' or, 'There it is!' because God's kingdom is within you.'" (New Century Version)

Remember that God is a Spirit and speaks inside you to your spirit. John 3:6–8 says, "⁶Human life comes from human parents, but spiritual life comes from the Spirit. ⁷Do not be surprised when I tell you, 'You must all be born again.' ⁸The wind blows where it wants to and you hear the sound of it, but you do not know where the wind comes from or where it is going. It is the same with every person who is born from the Spirit." God's spirit talks with you and to you. People around you who do not know God or hear His voice will see you doing things that make no sense to them but will then question why you seem to have so much peace, health, and prosperity. They will not be able to understand it. This is the light God speaks of that He wants you to shine on top of the hill. He wants everyone to come to know what Christ did for them and what He will do for you. Revelations 12:11 reads,

"And they overcame him because of the blood of the Lamb and because of the word of their testimony, and they did not love their life even when faced with death." You have overcome because of the blood of Christ, and the word of your testimony has more power than you know. It makes God real to yourself and to others, allowing not only yourself but also others to grow their hope placed in God to the point where not even death frightens them.

CHAPTER SEVEN

FAITH

What is it, really?

"Faith" can be an elusive word to understand. The devil has spent much of his existence keeping people from understanding this word. Hebrews 11:3 reads, "It is by faith we understand that the whole world was made by God's command so what we see was made by something that cannot be seen." (New Century Version) God, by His faith, created everything we can see in this world, and what we call "God's faith" comes from everything He says. Isaiah 55:10–11 states, "¹⁰For as the rain and the snow come down from heaven, and do not return there without watering the earth and making it bear and sprout, and furnishing seed to the sower and bread to the eater; ¹¹so will My word be which goes forth from My mouth; it will not return to Me empty, without accomplishing what I desire, and without succeeding in the matter for which I sent it." When God speaks, what is created from those words is real "faith," and we are able to use God's faith. His promise to us is that His words will come to pass.

Remember 1 Corinthians 13:13: "But now faith, hope, love, abide these three; but the greatest of these is love." These three things live, or *abide*, in today's world, or what God calls *this age*. There was a different age before Jesus came to Earth, and there will be another age when Christ returns. But until Jesus comes back, we are in the age of faith, hope, and love. We, as spiritual beings living in these fleshly, worldly bodies, can learn to live as Christ lived—in the manner God created us for—by living by God's definition of faith, hope, and love. Recall how we started with learning about love, the cornerstone of it all, which God showed through Jesus Christ. God forgave us of everything through Christ, His gift to us.

In this age, the Devil will do everything he can to keep you from realizing that you are able to spend time with, and talk to, God, every single day. Satan would much rather have you go back to your old, fallen way of thinking. The Devil will often try to keep you from going to God by reminding us of all of our shortcomings and how sinful we have been, but this will always be a lie, because God will love you, no matter what, and has always been, and will always be, there for you. 1 Corinthians 10:13 reads, "No temptation has overtaken you but such as is common to man; and God is faithful, who will not allow you to be tempted beyond what you are able, but with the temptation will provide the way of escape also, so that you will be able to endure it." Another great scripture on this subject can be found in Ephesians.

"¹In the past you were spiritually dead because of your sins and the things you did against God. ²Yes, in the past

you lived the way the world lives, following the ruler of the evil powers that are above the earth. That same spirit is now working in those who refuse to obey God. ³In the past all of us lived like them, trying to please our sinful selves and doing all the things our bodies and minds wanted. We should have suffered God's anger because we were sinful by nature. We were the same as all other people. ⁴But God's mercy is great, and He loves us very much. ⁵Though we were spiritually dead because of the things we did against God, He gave us new life with Christ. You have been saved by God's grace. ⁶And he raised us up with Christ and gave us a seat with Him in the heavens. He did this for those in Christ Jesus ⁷so that for all future time He could show the very great riches of His grace by being kind to us in Christ Jesus. ⁸I mean that you have been saved by grace through believing. You did not save yourselves; it was a gift from God. ⁹It was not the result of your own efforts, so you cannot brag about it. ¹⁰God has made us what we are. In Christ Jesus, God made us to do good works, which God planned in advance for us to live our lives doing."

—**Ephesians 2:1–10** (**New Century Version**)

The scripture above perfectly puts into words the gifts of love, hope, and faith that God gave to us. But what exactly does the Devil try to tell us the word "faith" means? Oftentimes, people believe that faith is an unknown, that we can never really be sure, because faith is just something inside of you that may or may not happen. Or they will believe that only God knows, and the extent of their faith is just hoping that it "may" happen. The confusion that the Devil tries to cause with this way of thinking causes people to think that there is the possibility that God will not stay faithful to us on His word. However, the Bible says that God's faith, or words, will always come to pass, that God will always be faithful to us. God's faith will always come to pass—you can be sure of it and have full hope in Him. This is how faith and hope relate. Hope is being sure of God coming through for us, and faith is staying loyal to that thought and hope. The Devil, for almost all of humanity's history, has taught us that faith is a game of chance, in which we end up losing most of the time, causing people not to trust God but to blame Him for everything. Remember that it is not God, but rather the Devil, that is here to kill, steal, and destroy. "A thief comes to steal and kill and destroy, but I came to give life—life in all its fullness. I am the good shepherd. The good shepherd gives his life for the sheep." (John 10:10–11, New Century Version) Always remember that God is for you and loves you so much that He sent His son that you may have life and have it abundantly.

It is all God. He removed the law that kept Him from coming to you because of your sins, past, present, and future. God removed all sin, through Jesus Christ, that would ever keep us apart from Him, and, because of this, we can now hear from Him all the time and receive faith to live a life with Him. The life that results from this is the life we were originally created for while we are here on this Earth. We all start our walk with God with misinformation from the world in our minds, through which He will slowly help us work out, with love. Little by little, He will show us the way to His love for us, and what is best for us, always following through with what He says to us as we walk with Him each day.

At its core, the gospel is this: God is with you right now, and He is no longer separated from you; He is able to speak to you at all times because of what He did in Christ Jesus. As you listen to Him, your relationship with Him grows. God's soft voice, inside you, gently tells you the little and great things that faith really is. It is completely God, His voice, speaking to you personally.

As we saw in Ephesians, no one is able to brag about being saved because it is a gift from God and not from our own actions. So why are we being told that we are not successful, or healed, because we lack faith? The Devil has twisted Romans 10:17: "So faith comes from hearing, and hearing by the word of Christ." We know that the Bible is the infallible word of God, but this often devolves into people picking any scripture they want and then demanding that God must perform it. This is simply not how it works, because God's faith is active and alive. Hebrews 4:12 says, "For the word of God is living and active and sharper than any two-edged sword, and piercing as far as the division of soul and spirit, of both joints and marrow, and able to judge the thoughts and intentions of the heart." This scripture is telling us that God will speak His word to us personally, inside of us, and the words He speaks to us is faith. We hear God's faith as He speaks to us, which is a substance greater than anything else in this world. It is the only real faith there is. This faith has the power to perform the work that God sends to us.

Understand that God is faithful to perform His word wherever He sends it, however, on this fallen Earth, there is a higher law. This "higher" law is one that even God cannot circumvent. Most people's first thought when hearing this is, "What? God is God, and He can do whatever He wants." This would be true if God were not faithful to His word and to love. Remember, we live in a time in which God has handed authority, the permission to rule, over to us, until this age is over and Jesus returns. Currently, we, as humans, have the final say on what happens here until Christ returns. Once Jesus comes back, He will be King of Kings and Lord of Lords. That is part of the reason there is such a battle over your mind and soul. God has given us the keys of authority over this Earth, and it is then up to us to either pick them up and use them for God or to hand those keys over to Satan, allowing him to rule over us.

God giving us authority over this Earth can be seen in the Bible as early as Genesis 1:26, which reads, "Then God said, 'Let Us make man in Our image, according to Our likeness; and let them rule over the fish of the sea and over the birds of the sky and over the cattle and over all the earth, and over every creeping thing that creeps on the earth.'" God specifically said, "Let them rule" over all of the entities of the Earth. This is a part of God's plan for this age. We, as humans, have the final say over what we allow on this Earth simply because God gave it to us. Satan understood this, which is why the first thing he did was get Adam and Eve to mistrust what God had said and instead trust what he was telling them. That has not changed, and the majority of the population on Earth today mistrusts what God is telling them, essentially handing their keys of authority over to Satan and being ruled by him.

Every day you wake up, you have to make a choice to either believe what God says or believe what the Devil says. We live in the Devil's world, his influence infecting our thoughts and desires, through almost everything around us: TV, radio, signs, other people and their thoughts, and ideas being spoken. But because of God's love, He sent Jesus, who paid the penalty of sin for us. Because of this love, we now have a chance, but it is up to us to choose who we believe. This choice is described in the Bible in both the Old and New Testaments.

*"*¹⁵*See, I have set before you today life and prosperity, and death and adversity;* ¹⁶*in that I command you today to love the Lord your God, to walk in His ways and to keep His commandments and His statutes and His judgements, that you may live and multiply, and that the Lord your God may bless you in the land where you are entering to possess it.* ¹⁷*But if your heart turns away and you will not obey, but are drawn away and worship other gods and serve them,* ¹⁸*I declare to you today that you shall surely perish. You will not prolong your days in the land where you are crossing the Jordan to enter and possess it.* ¹⁹*I call heaven and earth to witness against you today,*

that I have set before you life and death, the blessing and the curse. So choose life in order that you may live, you and your descendants, [20]by loving the Lord your God, by obeying His voice, and by holding fast to Him; for this is your life and the length of your days, that you may live in the land which the Lord swore to your fathers, to Abraham, Isaac, and Jacob, to give them.'"

—DEUTERONOMY 30:15-20

Notice how God specified to obey His voice and not to let our hearts turn away. God is referring to your inner spirit when He uses the word "heart." When you hear God speak inside of you, ask Him to show you what He is talking about in scripture. This is one of the fastest ways to start believing that voice is God. Once you realize it, as the scripture above says, do not turn away from it. The inner voice of God is life, and we have to choose to have it. If we reject the voice that brings life, then we choose death, just like Adam and Eve did in the Garden. Adam and Eve started life full of God and, by listening to one word from the Devil and believing that word over God's word, they lost it all. The opposite is true for us: We start this life full of the Devil's influence, but as soon as we listen to one word from God and believe that word over what the Devil is telling us, then the Devil loses influence over us. "For God so loved the world, that He gave His only begotten Son, that whoever believes in Him shall not perish, but have eternal life." (John 3:16).

God has given us authority over this Earth during this age. The Devil does not start with the authority, but millions of people are giving it to him each day. Remember that we have the final say over who our authority is given to—it all depends on who we choose to listen to and follow on this Earth. Jesus speaks of this in John 3:14–21, saying, "[14]As Moses lifted up the serpent in the wilderness, even so must the Son of Man be lifted up; [15]so that whoever believes in Him will have eternal life. [16]"For God so loved the world that He gave His only begotten Son, that whoever believes in Him shall not perish, but have eternal life. [17]For God did not send the Son into the world to judge the world, but that the world might be saved through Him. [18]He who believes in Him is not judged; he who does not believe has been judged already, because he has not believed in the name of the only begotten Son of God. [19]This is the judgement, that the Light has come into the world, and men loved the darkness rather than the Light, for their deeds were evil. [20]For everyone who does evil hates the Light, and does not come to the Light for fear that his deeds will be exposed. [21]But he who practices the truth comes to the Light, so that his deeds may be manifested as having been wrought in God.'"

There is so much to unpack in the scripture above, however, it all boils down to the same concept: that it is up to us to decide. The more we practice the truth, God's voice and truth, the more our mind becomes renewed. We begin to recognize and believe God's voice quicker when He speaks to us. That inner voice, in our spirit, is who God created us to believe. It is the real you, the one born again, recreated by God, for eternal living. This is seen in James 1:21–25: "[21]Therefore, putting aside all filthiness and all that remains of wickedness, in humility receive the word implanted, which is able to save your souls. ²²But prove yourselves doers of the word, and not merely hearers who delude themselves. ²³For if anyone is a hearer of the word and not a doer, he is like a man who looks at his natural face in a mirror; ²⁴for once he has looked at himself and gone away, he has immediately forgotten what kind of person he was. ²⁵But one who looks intently at the perfect law, the law of liberty, and abides by it, not having become a forgetful hearer but an effectual doer, this man will be blessed in what he does." This is the Holy Spirit showing you who you truly are. Your real life is the voice of God inside of you, the eternal you. When you hear His voice, choose to act on it. The abundant life that God is trying to give you lies in listening to, and acting on, this voice. The only thing standing in the way of abundant life is you, stopping yourself with the knowledge and doubt that the world has poured into you. When you listen and act on His voice inside of you, you will be blessed—blessed not *sometimes*, but *all the time.*

Here are some of God's faith-producing words from Deuteronomy 28:1–14:

""¹Now it shall be, if you diligently obey the Lord your God, being careful to do all His commandments which I command you today, the Lord your God will set you high above all the nations of the earth. ²All these bless-ings will come upon you and overtake you if you obey the Lord your God:

³Blessed shall you be in the city, and blessed shall you be in the country.

⁴Blessed shall be the offspring of your body and the produce of your ground and the offspring of your beasts, the increase of your herd and the young of your flock.

⁵Blessed shall be your basket and your kneading bowl.

⁶Blessed shall you be when you come in, and blessed shall you be when you go out.

⁷The Lord shall cause your enemies who rise up against you to be defeated before you; they will come out against you one way and flee before you seven ways. ⁸The Lord will command the blessing upon you in your barns and in all that you put your hand to, and He will bless you in the land which the Lord your God gives you. ⁹The Lord will establish you as a holy people to Himself, as He swore to you, if you keep the commandments of the Lord your God and walk in His ways. ¹⁰So all the peoples of the earth will see that you are called by the name of the Lord, and they will be afraid of you. ¹¹The Lord will make you abound in prosperity, in the offspring of your body and in the offspring of your beast and in the produce of your ground, in the land which the Lord swore to your fathers to give you. ¹²The Lord will open for you His good storehouse, the heavens, to give rain to your land in its season and to bless all the work of your hand; and you shall lend to many nations, but you shall not borrow. ¹³*The Lord will make you the head and not the tail, and you only will be above, and you will not be underneath, if you listen to the commandments of the Lord your God, which I charge you today, to observe them carefully,* ¹⁴*and do not turn aside from any of the words which I command you today, to the right or to the left, to go after other gods to serve them."'*

Listen to the voice of His Spirit, which is inside of you, and do what He asks you in your spirit. Every single person has their own journey with God, a different plan for each person. Do not get into the mindset that the scripture above means that you will be blessed only if you observe all the Old Covenant laws; this is incorrect thinking. Instead, understand that Jesus fulfilled the Old Covenant law and has now given us the Holy Spirit, so that we now receive God's blessing when we act on the things that God personally asks us to do.

CHAPTER EIGHT

HEBREWS 11

Adding your name

As I briefly mentioned in the discussion of the word "hope" in previous chapters, Hebrews 11 is known for its examples of faith. Now that we have delved into faith, hope, and love, we need to take a closer look at this chapter. Hebrews 11:1 reads, "Now faith is the reality of what is hoped for, the proof of what is not seen" (Christian Standard Bible). When you hear from God yourself, it is at that moment that spiritual faith enters into you. Be completely sure in your spirit that what God said will come to pass, even when your mind tries to reject it with what the world has taught you. The more you practice this, the easier it becomes. Jeremiah 33:3 reads, "Call to Me and I will answer you, and I will tell you great and mighty things, which you do not know." When we step out with God and follow His steps to accomplish the things set before us, the world will take notice that you are doing something different—and that it's working.

Hebrews 11:2 says, "For by it (faith received from hearing God) our ancestors won God's approval" (Christian Standard

Bible). It's simple: We can live in the kingdom of God today, and this is actually how you and I are supposed to live during our short time here on Earth. Jesus said this in Revelations 12:11: "And they overcame him because of the blood of the Lamb and because of the word of their testimony, and they did not love their life even when faced with death." Jesus's death is the blood of the Lamb, and your part is to have a testimony that comes from hearing God yourself and acting on what that small voice inside of you is saying.

When I first started walking with Christ, I used to read this Revelations verse and always get stuck on the phrase, "they did not love their life even when faced with death." Personally, I know several great men of God who were imprisoned and tortured for their faith in, and love of, Jesus Christ. The thought of that happening to me or a loved one scared me, and it still does. However, as I have grown closer to God over all these years, He brought me back to this verse and reminded me of the first line in it: "they did not love their life." This thought goes against everything that this world has taught us to know. Imagine being in such a close relationship with the God who created everything around you that even death does not scare you. Paul displays this in 2 Corinthians 5:1–2 when he says, "¹We know that our body—the tent we live in here on earth—will be destroyed. But when that happens, God will have a house for us. It will not be a house made by human hands; instead, it will be a home in heaven that will last forever. ²But now we groan in this tent. We want God to give us our heavenly home." Paul continues on, talking about the difference between our earthly body and our heavenly body, all the while recognizing that, even while on Earth, we long to be in heaven. It is OK to still be afraid of death; we all are until we grow even deeper in our relationship with God. Remember that it is a process, and every single person, Paul included, had to grow and learn along the way to reach this point.

Even throughout all of Hebrews 11, all the great men and women of God who accomplished so much on this Earth did so simply by hearing from God personally and doing it. Their stories always end with them gaining a testimony through their faith but not receiving the main promise, which is the promise of the resurrection of our bodies. "[39]And all these, having gained approval through their faith, did not receive what was promised, because [40]God had provided something better for us, so that apart from us they would not be made perfect" (Hebrews 11:39–40). All of us together will be made perfect, and as you grow with Christ, He will reveal more of this in greater detail.

There are many people of great faith mentioned in chapter 11 of Hebrews. Remember that it is God Who does everything. All we have to do, and all these people had to do, was simply listen and obey. Some of the people of great faith mentioned in chapter 11 of Hebrews are:

Hebrews 11:7: *"By faith Noah, being warned by God about things not yet seen, in reverence prepared an ark for the salvation of his household, by which he condemned the* *world, and became an heir of the righteousness which is according to faith."*

This verse is referencing chapter 6 in Genesis, when God tells Noah to build an ark. Genesis 6:13–14: "¹³Then God said to Noah, 'The end of all flesh has come before Me; for the earth is filled with violence because of them; and behold, I am about to destroy them with the earth. ¹⁴Make for yourself an ark of gopher wood; you shall make the ark with rooms, and shall cover it inside and out with pitch."

The rest of the chapter goes into detail on how exactly God wanted the ark built, and Noah listened, which saved him and his family from death.

Hebrews 11:8–10: *"⁸By faith Abraham, when he was called, obeyed by going out to a place which he was to receive for an inheritance; and he went out, not knowing where he was going. ⁹By faith he lived as an alien in the land of promise, as in a foreign land, dwelling in tents with Isaac and Jacob, fellow heirs of the same promise; ¹⁰for he was looking for the city which has foundations, whose architect and builder is God."*

This is referencing Genesis chapter 12:1–4, when God asked Abraham to leave his land and family behind, and to follow Him. "¹Now the Lord said to Abram, 'Go forth from your country, and from your relatives, and from your father's house, to the land which I will show you; ²and I will make you a great nation, and I will bless you, and make your name great; and so you shall be a blessing; ³and I will bless those who bless you, and the one who curses you I will curse. And in you all the families of the earth will be blessed.' ⁴So Abram went forth as the Lord had spoken to him; and Lot went with him. Now Abram was seventy-five years old when he departed from Haran."

Abraham simply left and went where God directed him because the Lord had spoken it to him. In our lives, it is OK to ask God for confirmation, either through scripture or another spirit-filled Christian, but the core of everything is simply listening to what God is telling you and then doing it. Remember, God's spoken words to you is the real faith, and when you believe and act on it, that is God's righteousness. This can be seen in Genesis 15:6: "Then he believed in the Lord; and He reckoned it to him as righteousness."

Hebrews 11:11–12: *"¹¹By faith even Sarah herself received ability to conceive, even beyond the proper time of life, since she considered Him faithful who had promised. ¹²Therefore, there was born even of one man, and him as good as dead at that, as many descendants as the stars of heaven in number, and innumerable as the sand which is by the seashore." This is referencing Genesis 18:10–14: When God was speaking to Abraham, "He said, 'I will surely return to you at this time next year; and behold, Sarah your wife will have a son.' And Sarah was listening at the tent door, which was behind him. Now Abraham and Sarah were old, advanced in age; Sarah was past* *childbearing. Sarah laughed to herself, saying, 'After I have become old, shall I have pleasure, my lord being old also?' And the Lord said to Abraham, 'Why did Sarah laugh, saying, 'Shall I indeed bear a child, when I am so old?' Is anything too difficult for the Lord? At the appointed time I will return to you, at this time next year, and Sarah will have a son.'"*

The Lord did not hide His plans from Abraham or Sarah. This is seen in Genesis 18:17–19: "¹⁷The Lord said, 'Shall I hide from Abraham what I am about to do, ¹⁸since Abraham will surely become a great and mighty nation, and in him all the nations of the earth will be blessed? ¹⁹For I have chosen him, so that he may command his children and his household after him to keep the way of the Lord by doing righteousness and justice, so that the Lord may bring upon Abraham what He has spoken about him.'"

The Lord did not do this only for Abraham and Sarah. God continues to keep every person whom He speaks to informed on His plans. It is not God's will for us as Christians to be kept in the dark, grabbing at straws, trying to do the right thing. Rather God is transparent with us about where He is leading us, and all we have to do is listen and obey each step He gives us along the way.

Hebrews chapter 11 goes on to talk about Moses, Joseph, Jacob, Isaac, Gideon, Samson, Jephthah, David, Samuel, and many of the prophets, all of whom were made great by faith.

They all gained a testimony by their faith. Each of these people had God personally speak to them, and, by believing God's words, they created righteousness in themselves, giving them the ability to overcome the enemy. By listening to God and acting on His words, they were able to break the plans of the Devil. You and I are no different from everyone mentioned in Hebrews 11. We all have the same ability to listen to God and do what He asks. The difference comes down to whether you follow God's voice or not.

All of these great men and women of faith heard personally from God, believed it, acted on it, and, as a result, God was pleased. However, do you see anywhere in the Bible where one of these people of faith began reading history books about other great people of faith who lived before them and say to themselves, "I must copy them exactly, because the scripture says that God does not change. So, if it worked for them, then it must work for me." Did any of them copy Noah and build an ark? Did any of them act like Gideon and take a group of men down to the river to see who of those drank using their hands in order to pick men for an army? No, of course not. Many people in today's world will try to copy exactly what people in the Bible did and then blame God when they do not get the same results. This does not work because God gives every single person something different, designed for each individual. You are not meant to be walking someone else's path of faith with God, because He has made a path especially for you.

We are extremely lucky to live in the age after Christ's crucifixion and resurrection. Jesus said in Matthew 11:11, "Truly

I say to you, among those born of women there has not arisen anyone greater than John the Baptist! Yet the one who is the least in the kingdom of heaven is greater than he." That is us. By hearing and obeying God's voice, we are citizens of the kingdom of heaven. This is God's gift to us, not earned from what we have done, but rather because of what Jesus did for us.

We are so extremely lucky, or as the Bible says, "blessed." We are abundantly blessed to hear His voice for ourselves. Hearing God's voice and acting on it is salvation, which we need every single day. Paul says this as well in Romans 10:1–13, when he attempts to tell people that they no longer have to live under the rules of the past but that there is a new way which comes by receiving the direct source of God Himself.

"¹Brethren, my heart's desire and my prayer to God for them is for their salvation. ²For I testify about them that they have a zeal for God, but not in accordance with knowledge. ³For not knowing about God's righteousness and seeking to establish their own, they did not subject themselves to the righteousness of God. ⁴For Christ is the end of the law for righteousness to everyone who believes. ⁵For Moses writes that the man who practices the righteousness which is based on law shall live by that righteousness. ⁶But the righteousness based on faith speaks as follows: 'Do not say in your heart, 'Who will ascend into heaven?' (that is, to bring Christ down), ⁷or 'Who will descend into the abyss?' (that is, to bring Christ up from the dead). ⁸But what does it say? 'The word is near

you, in your mouth and in your heart.' That is, the word of faith which we are preaching, ⁹that if you confess with your mouth Jesus as Lord, and believe in your heart that God raised Him from the dead, you will be saved; ¹⁰for with the heart a person believes, resulting in righteousness, and with the mouth he confesses, resulting in salvation. ¹¹For the Scripture says, 'Whoever believes in Him will not be disappointed.' ¹²For there is no distinction between Jew and Greek; for the same Lord is Lord of all, abounding in riches for all who call on Him; ¹³for 'Whoever will call on the name of the Lord will be saved.'"

In verse 1, Paul is speaking about the Jewish people and the way they continue to live and behave, not understanding what Christ has done, continuing with all of the old laws and rituals. In verse 3, he recalls that God's righteousness is when we personally hear His voice and act on it. Verse 4 is extremely important in this scripture. Remember how seriously God takes what you believe in your heart, because this is where the power of salvation lies. We originally lost it all when Adam and Eve believed Satan, however, now God has made it easier than ever to regain a relationship with Him. All we have to do is believe what God did in Christ, and it is finished. We just have to thank God in our hearts for what he did in and through Jesus Christ.

In verses 5–8 Paul leads us through several rhetorical questions and ends with asking us what it really says. Read the scripture above again, and ask yourself, "What is it really saying?" Try to come up with an answer for yourself. It is so easy to simply continue reading and get the answer that Paul gives to us, however, it is important to conclude it for yourself in your heart so that it rings true for you personally. Verses 8–10 talk about "the word' that is near to us, which is God's voice. When verse 10 says, "for with the heart a person believes," it is referring to when the person personally hears God speak to them and believes that it is indeed God's voice within themselves. Remember Abraham from the Old Testament; when he believed what God had said, God accounted that as righteousness. Understand that salvation is not just going to heaven; instead, it is also salvation from the cares and troubles of this world.

Since we are saved from the cares and troubles of this world, with God walking right next to us each and every day, we can rest assured that He always hears us. Always remember that God is in you and with you. Oftentimes, we will reach out to Jesus only when we are already in over our heads and need help. We cry out to Jesus, who is seated on the throne in heaven next to God. However, it is the Holy Spirit inside of you who is getting the direct words from Jesus and giving them to you. We have to listen to the still, small voice of God through the Holy Spirit inside of us in order to get the help we so often cry out for. The words of God that we reach for daily is Christ, and Jesus is the living embodiment of the Word, God's word.

God is desperately trying to speak to us, and all we have to do is call on Him. Breaking away from this and trying to use our own mind to distinguish, or judge, between good and evil is what hinders all of this. This is something Paul fought throughout the Bible. One of the places Paul brings attention to this is in Galatians 3:1–9:

"¹You foolish Galatians! Who has bewitched you? Before your very eyes Jesus Christ was clearly portrayed as crucified. ²I would like to learn just one thing from you: Did you receive the Spirit by the works of law, or by believing what you heard? ³Are you so foolish? After beginning by means of the Spirit, are you now trying to finish by means of the flesh? ⁴Have you experienced so much in vain—if it really was in vain? ⁵So again I ask, does God give you His Spirit and work miracles among you by the works of the law, or by your believing what you heard? ⁶So also Abraham 'believed God, and it was credited to him as righteousness.' ⁷Understand, then, that those who have faith are children of Abraham. ⁸Scripture foresaw that God would justify the Gentiles by faith and announced the gospel in advance to Abraham: 'All nations will be blessed through you.' ⁹So those who rely on faith are blessed along with Abraham, the man of faith" (New International Version).

This is why it is so important to hear God's voice and have a deep understanding that God wants to help us in all areas of our lives. We are not meant to be the judge and earn righteousness through our own works. Instead, we are meant to live in relationship with God, Who is not there just for major events or choices but rather for everything we do. God does not limit Himself. This is part of the reason I spoke about how our mind does its best to destroy or confuse the word God gives to us, clouding up its power and causing His words not to perform as intended because we get in the way of ourselves.

Look at Romans 14:23. Paul is correcting people because they are arguing over what the Bible's rules were for eating; Paul corrects them, showing us that everything is now through God. "But he who doubts is condemned if he eats, because his eating is not from faith; and whatever is not from faith is sin." Remember that this verse is written to men and women who wish to serve God, revealing that, even when we are saved through the Blood of Christ, we all have battles with the sinful flesh that still lives within us. The more we fight and win each battle with our flesh, it clears out more space for God's spirit to live within us. However, the fight never seems to end, which is why we must learn to lean fully on Christ and on God's voice, inside of us at all times.

This battle is an eternal war within every single person that, with Christ, we will overcome. Here is an example of this that the Lord shared with me.

In the beginning there were two special trees, the tree of life and the tree of the knowledge of good and evil. To this day, everyone still has these two trees in their spirit. It all lies in how you view the Bible when you read it. Both of these trees were real, living trees in the Garden. God asked where paper comes from, which is trees. God continued by saying, "So a Bible is made from a tree, essentially the same material that in the beginning either held life or the knowledge of good and evil, and spiritually it is the same today." How do you approach the written word of God? Do you read it with eyes of the flesh, looking only for what is right or wrong so that you can have a better understanding of good and evil? Or do you read it looking for everlasting life, which is in Jesus Christ?

The whole Bible is made to point you to life everlasting, which is in Christ Jesus, but now God wants to put that same life in you. Jesus says in John 5:39–40, "³⁹You search the Scriptures because you think that in them you have eternal life; it is these that testify about Me; ⁴⁰and you are unwilling to come to Me so that you may have life." It is so simple that it can be hard to fully grasp. The cross we are supposed to carry is that same cross that Jesus has already carried for us. We can do nothing by our own Earthly wisdom and knowledge because it is all based in sin, the original sin of eating of the tree of knowledge of good and evil. The more we base our values and opinions on our worldly knowledge of good and evil, the further we are from the will of God. It is all God, and all we have to do is listen to what He says and how He judges. Jesus showed us that this is how we are supposed to live on this Earth now that the Holy Spirit is living inside of us. Jesus said, while referring to living on the earth and in the flesh, "I can do nothing on My own initiative. As I hear, I judge; and My judgment is just, because I do not seek my own will, but the will of Him who sent Me" (John 5:30).

This is how you and I are created to live. It is God's blessing on us that we are able to be His children and rely on Him in everything we do, which gives us His peace and prosperity. God has given us the right to be a brother or sister to Jesus. John 1:12–13 reads, "¹²But as many received Him, to them He gave the right to become children of God, even to those who believe in His name, ¹³who were born, not of blood nor of the will of the flesh nor of the will of man, but of God." When we hear His voice in us, this is God's will for us. God is speaking to your newly created, born-again spirit, which is who you truly are.

CHAPTER NINE

THE OLD IS
AN EXAMPLE

Don't end up short of God's rest

As a new creation in Christ, we are to live life by faith in every way. Remember that faith is God talking directly to you. God lives within you, His spirit talking with yours. 2 Corinthians 5:16–21 reads, "[16]Therefore from now on we recognize no one according to the flesh; even though we have known Christ according to the flesh, yet now we know Him in this way no longer. [17]Therefore if anyone is in Christ, he is a new creature; the old things passed away; behold, new things have come. [18]Now all these things are from God, who reconciled us to Himself through Christ and gave us the ministry of reconciliation, [19]namely, that God was in Christ reconciling the world to Himself, not counting their trespasses against them, and He has committed to us the word of reconciliation. [20]Therefore, we are ambassadors for Christ, as though God were making an appeal through us; we beg you on behalf of Christ, be reconciled to God. [21]He made Him who knew no sin to be sin on our behalf, so that we might become the righteousness of God in Him." Now that God has made us righteous, we can hear and understand Him. It is only our non-renewed mind, the flesh that still lives in us, that wants to argue and combat everything He tells us. It is all new to us, and, in general, we are all hesitant when it comes to something new at first, but after a while we realize that this is a positive thing and will become accustomed to it.

It will always be a growing process. The more we believe what God says and act on it, seeing that it actually works out, the more we believe that it is His spirit inside of us. This grows until we believe His spirit more than what our flesh is trying to tell us through the knowledge the world has taught us. This process is what God refers to as "crucifying the flesh." Galatians 5:24–25 reads, "²⁴Now those who belong to Christ Jesus have crucified the flesh with its passions and desires. ²⁵If we live by the Spirit, let us also walk by the Spirit." It is important to remember that the Bible was not originally written in English, and, as a result, it is often helpful to look up the key words that God has highlighted to you in the original language. This will often give deeper meaning and understanding to the verse and what God is trying to point out to you. In this scripture, the Greek for the word "crucify" is *stauroo*, which has two meanings. One meaning is the literal action of the Romans crucifying Christ on the cross. The other meaning is used figuratively as putting the old self to death by submitting all decisions and desires to the Lord (Strong's Numbers 4717, Greek). This means that we cannot walk with

God and still choose to live independently from Him. Also in this verse, the word "flesh" in the Greek definition is "carnal, merely of human origin or empowerment." (Strong's Number 4561, Greek). Finally, the word "passion" in the verses above, in the Greek definition, means, "the capacity to feel strong emotion, like suffering, properly, the capacity and privilege of experiencing strong feeling; felt, deep emotion, like agony, passion, etc." (Strong's Numbers 3804, Greek).

Looking at the previous verses, it is easy to see how much of a war is going on inside of each and every person. As soon as the Holy Spirit speaks to your spirit, the Devil immediately comes in and tries to put a stop to the word of God entering into the world. It is always up to us to whom we choose to listen. Joshua 24:14–16 reads, "'14Now, therefore, fear the Lord and serve Him in sincerity and truth; and put away the gods which your fathers served beyond the River and in Egypt, and serve the Lord. 15If it is disagreeable in your sight to serve the Lord, choose for yourselves today whom you will serve: whether the gods which your fathers served which were beyond the River, or the gods of the Amorites in whose land you are living; but as for me and my house, we will serve the Lord.' 16The people answered and said, 'Far be it from us that we should forsake the Lord to serve other gods.'" Do not let yourself get caught up in all the rules of the Old Testament scriptures. Many people hear the words "serve" and "fear" and choose to rebel against these things. But do not forget that you are a son or daughter of God, and God wants you to see that He is good. "O taste and see that the Lord is good; how blessed is the man who takes refuge in Him!" (Psalms 34:8). It is a journey with Him, and He will show you that He is good. The more you see and experience this, the more trusting you become, until you agree with Him that you should respect, or fear, Him more than you respect, or fear, what the world has taught you. You will come to realize that, every time you listen to God, it turns out well for you, and every time you listen to what the world has taught you, no matter how good it may feel at the time, it will end with you feeling ashamed and miserable.

King David fully realized how good God was, and trusted in Him fully. He wrote the Psalms through the inspiration of the Holy Spirit, and even though David was a king, he still contributed it all to God. This is a good example for us that, no matter how powerful you become here on Earth, it is all thanks to God.

"¹I will bless the Lord at all times; His praise shall continually be in my mouth. ²My soul will make its boast in the Lord; the humble will hear it and rejoice. ³O magnify the Lord with me, and let us exalt His name together. ⁴I sought the Lord, and He answered me, and delivered me from all my fears. ⁵They looked to Him and were radiant, and their faces will never be ashamed. ⁶This poor man cried, and the Lord heard him and saved him out of all his troubles. ⁷The angel of the Lord encamps around those who fear Him, and rescues them. ⁸O taste and see that the Lord is good; how blessed is the man who takes refuge in Him! ⁹O fear the Lord, you His saints; for to

those who fear Him there is no want. [10]The young lions do lack and suffer hunger; but they who seek the Lord shall not be in want of any good thing. [11]Come, you children, listen to me; I will teach you the fear of the Lord. [12]Who is the man who desires life and loves length of days that he may see good? [13]Keep your tongue from evil and your lips from speaking deceit. [14]Depart from evil and do good; seek peace and pursue it. [15]The eyes of the Lord are toward the righteous and His ears are open to their cry. [16]The face of the Lord is against evildoers, to cut off the memory of them from the earth. [17]The righteous cry, and the Lord hears and delivers them out of all their troubles. [18]The Lord is near to the brokenhearted and saves those who are crushed in spirit. [19]Many are the afflictions of the righteous, but the Lord delivers him out of them all. [20]He keeps all his bones, not one of them is broken. [21]Evil shall slay the wicked, and those who hate the righteous will be condemned. [22]The Lord redeems the soul of His servants, and none of those who take refuge in Him will be condemned."

—PSALMS 34

Did you notice in the verses above that there is nothing about having to wait until you die to be with God? God wants to save you today! We are meant to have God's kingdom here on Earth, not just when we die and go to heaven. In Matthew 6:9–13, Jesus's disciples asked him how to pray, and He responded with what many know today as the Lord's prayer. "⁹Pray, then, in this way: 'Our Father who is in heaven, hallowed be Your name. ¹⁰Your kingdom come, Your will be done, on earth as it is in heaven. ¹¹Give us this day our daily bread. ¹²And forgive us our debts, as we also have forgiven our debtors. ¹³And do not lead us into temptation, but deliver us from evil. [For Yours is the kingdom and the power and the glory forever. Amen]'" Take special notice of verse 10, "Your kingdom come, Your will be done, on earth as it is in heaven." We are to ask for God's Kingdom to come to Earth.

Today, if you hear his voice, do not harden your heart to it, because this is how God's Kingdom can be brought to Earth in this age. Hebrews 3:15–19 reads, "'¹⁵Today if you hear His voice, do not harden your hearts, as when they provoked Me.' ¹⁶For who provoked Him when they had heard? Indeed, did not all those who came out of Egypt led by Moses? ¹⁷And with whom was He angry for forty years? Was it not with those who sinned, whose bodies fell in the wilderness? ¹⁸And to whom did He swear that they would not enter His rest, but to those who were disobedient? ¹⁹So we see that they were not able to enter because of unbelief." God sent Jesus as the sacrifice for our sins so that we could have the Holy Spirit, God's voice, inside of us. When we listen to Him and do what He asks, we are able to enter His rest and have the peace in our lives as God promises us.

It is in this age that we are to listen to God and bring His kingdom to Earth. 1 Corinthians 10:11 reads, "Now these things happened to them as an example, and they were written for our instruction, upon whom the ends of the ages have come."

We are truly blessed to be living in the last age before Christ returns. God paid such a great price when he sent Jesus to the Earth. Make sure not to live as they did before Christ came and died on the cross, following all the rules but still coming short of the righteousness of God. Rather, live as God meant us to live from the start by simply listening to and following Him—a new way to live where we can be in fellowship with Him at all times.

CHAPTER TEN

TITHING

You are free in Christ alone

So far, we have learned that God is love, which is shown best in Jesus Christ. We have learned that the whole purpose of Jesus's crucifixion and rising from the dead was so that God could legally defeat the Devil and regain access to speak to us. We have come to see that it is God who did all this through Jesus Christ and that there was no way we could have done it ourselves. Ephesians 2:8–10 reads, "⁸For by grace you have been saved through faith; and that not of yourselves, it is the gift of God; ⁹not as a result of works, so that no one may boast. ¹⁰For we are His workmanship, created in Christ Jesus for good works, which God prepared beforehand so that we would walk in them."

We are saved through faith when we personally hear from God and act on it. God's word that we hear and act on saves us from the pain and suffering, mentally and physically, that this world tries to put on us. By ourselves, we are unable to achieve this through our own works, done outside of faith. Remember that everything not done in faith is sin. Romans 14:23 says,

"But he who doubts is condemned if he eats, because his eating is not from faith; and whatever is not from faith is sin." Praise the Lord that we are forgiven of our sins, past, present, and future, and that God gives us unlimited amounts of grace!

Working with faith can also be related to tithing. The subject of tithing causes contention in many Christian communities; it is even used as a reason not to become a Christian. Many Christians tithe for the sole reason of expecting blessings from God because of their tithing. It seems like tithing is one of the biggest things that many churches refuse to give to God, to release it from their own control, and let God direct it. The Devil has snuck into many churches' teachings on tithing, adding into the redemption and loving God, that it is not only what Jesus did on the cross, but also you giving "at least" ten percent of your earnings. By tithing at least this amount you, the Devil says, you will be able to gain access to God and be totally released from His anger. This is a lie of the Devil! It is a lie that needs to be brought into the light by churches around the world and addressed. Think back to the thief on the cross beside Jesus, who simply believed that He was the son of God and because of this, he saw Jesus that same day in heaven. Remember the Holy Spirit inside of you is everything. When we die and stand before Him, obeying God and how we walked in His kingdom here on Earth is all He is going to care about. Jesus said in Matthew 7:21, "Not everyone who says to Me, 'Lord, Lord,' will enter the kingdom of heaven, but he who does the will of My Father who is in heaven will enter."

As we have discussed, the Old Testament is full of rules that were originally designed before we were cleansed with the blood of Christ and able to come freely before the throne of God, to show us that we could not keep them fully. God purposely showed us these rules to help us understand that we needed a savior, which only He could supply through Jesus Christ. Now, after the cross, we have only two rules, which are written in Matthew 22:37–40: "³⁷And He said to him, 'You shall the love the Lord your God with all your heart, and with all your soul, and with all your mind.' ³⁸This is the great and foremost commandment. ³⁹The second is like it, 'You shall love your neighbor as yourself.' ⁴⁰On these two commandments depend the whole Law and the Prophets." Many people read these verses and argue that, because Jesus tells us to love Him with all our heart, soul, and mind, this means doing what He says, and He specifically says in the Old Testament that not tithing is stealing from God. "'Bring the whole tithe into the storehouse, so that there may be food in My house, and test me now in this,' says the Lord of hosts, 'if I will not open for you the windows of heaven and pour out for you a blessing until it overflows.'" (Malachi 3:10). They will continue to argue, pointing out that Jesus said to tithe in the New Testament. But did He really? Luke 11:42 reads, "But woe to you Pharisees! For you pay tithe of mint and rue and every kind of garden herb, and yet disregard justice and the love of God; but these are the things you should have done without neglecting the others." Notice that Jesus said that the Pharisees, the keepers of the Old Testament law, were disregarding the love of God by following the rules written in the Old Testament. Does this mean we can completely disregard the Old Testament and go out and do what we want? Absolutely not! If we are pursuing a relationship with God, and loving God and others, then how could we steal from people, or commit other sins against them?

Out of all the rules the Bible has placed on us, tithing is the one rule that the church refuses to let go of when it comes to receiving blessings from God. But remember that Jesus told the Pharisees that they were disregarding the love of God. They, the keepers of the Law, bypassed this love by tithing. Remember that Jesus was talking to these Pharisees before He was crucified, releasing us from the Old Testament laws. Some scriptures that support this are: 2 Corinthians 5:17, "Therefore if anyone is in Christ, he is a new creature; the old things passed away; behold, new things have come." Isaiah 43:18, "Do not call to mind the former things, or ponder things of the past." Galatians 6:15, "For neither is circumcision anything, nor uncircumcision, but a new creation." Hebrews 8:13, "When He said, 'A new covenant,' He has made the first obsolete. But whatever is becoming obsolete and growing old is ready to disappear."

Being held captive by one Old Testament rule, such as tithing, in order to receive blessings and peace from God is a slippery slope. There will always be one more thing you have to do to be made right with God when you rely on the old law. Remember that our redemption is from God. 2 Corinthians 3:5–6 reads, "⁵Not that we are adequate in ourselves to consider anything as coming from ourselves, but our adequacy is from God, ⁶who also made us adequate as servants of a new covenant, not of the letter but of the Spirit; for the letter kills, but the Spirit gives life." We live after the cross, and because of this, we get to live a victorious life that many people in the Old Testament only dreamed about. "No one puts new wine into old wineskins; otherwise the wine will burst the skins, and the wine is lost and the skins as well; but one puts new wine into fresh wineskins." (Mark 2:22). We must shed our old wineskin, the one ruled by Old Testament law and the world, and, as we become a new creation in Christ, put on a fresh wineskin. Every time we try to mix the new covenant of the New Testament with the rules and laws of the Old Testament, we are bursting our newly created spirits and giving up all that Christ has done for us. Take a moment to quiet yourself and see what God has to say on this matter Himself.

I pray that, at this point, you have realized that hearing from God yourself and acting on those words is how we are meant to live in this age. Jesus's spirit, or the Holy Spirit, living within us is the eternal life that Jesus so often tries to explain to His disciples. We must read the word of God with His Spirit revealing His message for us and explaining things we come across that our flesh tries to fight. Jesus says in Matthew 11:28–30, "²⁸Come to Me, all who are weary and heavy laden, and I will give you rest. ²⁹Take My yoke upon you and learn from Me, for I am gentle and humble in heart, and you will find rest for your souls. ³⁰For My yoke is easy and My burden is light." Jesus also says in John 14:26–27, "²⁶But the Helper, the Holy Spirit, whom the Father will send in My name, He will teach you all things, and bring to your remembrance all that I said to you. ²⁷Peace I leave with you; My peace I give to you; not as the world gives do I give to you. Do not let your heart be troubled, nor let it be fearful."

With these words of Jesus in mind, think to yourself: *Am I tithing out of fear—fear that, if I do not tithe, God is going to curse me?* Galatians 3:11–14 sheds light on this: "¹¹Now that no one is justified by the Law before God is evident; for, 'The righteous man shall live by faith.' ¹²However, the Law is not of faith; on the contrary, 'He who practices them shall live by them.' ¹³Christ redeemed us from the curse of the Law, having become a curse for us—for it is written, 'Cursed is everyone who hangs" on a tree"—¹⁴in order that, in Christ Jesus, the blessing of Abraham might come to the Gentiles, so that we would receive the promise of the Spirit through faith." Jesus saved us from the curse of the old law, so that now, when we have a relationship with Him, we are freed from it. Only through faith, hearing God's words and receiving them, can we have complete confidence in his goodness. Jesus says in Mark 10:18, "Why do you call Me good? No one is good except God alone."

Understand that we are not created to serve two masters, and that we cannot serve God and money at the same time. Matthew 6:24 reads, "No one can serve two masters; for either he will hate the one and love the other, or he will be devoted to one and despise the other. You cannot serve God and wealth." Does this mean that you never have to tithe again? No, it does not. It simply means that you are no longer a slave to tithing in order to gain God's blessings. Instead, if God speaks to you and asks you to give, then give. Do not feel pressured to give more or less than what God is asking you. Even if you ask Him about giving and He says that you do not have to give anything, do not be pressured into giving. It is all up to God and us listening to Him. So, right now, I say, in the name of Jesus Christ, be set free from the slavery of tithing, and walk in the freedom of Christ Jesus.

CHAPTER ELEVEN

GOD'S WISDOM

His Spirit wars against your knowledge

A question that I often hear is, "Why does God work so strongly in some people's lives but not in mine?" or "I see great men and women of God living the way I wish to live, but when I do what they say, I am not seeing the same results as them. Then I am told I need more faith, which, they say, is in the form of sacrificing something to them, and they show it scripturally in the Bible, so it must be true." Honestly, things similar to this *are* in the Bible, but if you act on what they say, it will not work for you. This is because it is only true faith that is guaranteed to work all the time. It is the faith that comes from the words God has spoken directly to you, not the words that men or women tell you.

Another thing people often question is why we are here on this Earth. Personally, figuring this out took me a while to understand, because it mixes all of the lessons I have mentioned in this book. The Holy Spirit had been speaking to me for around six years about drinking alcohol. I prayed again and again, asking why He would not take the spirit of joy and fun out of drinking, like He did many years before with marijuana. I knew what His will was, and when I failed, I felt so convicted and would always defend myself with all the scriptures on how drinking in the Bible was OK. This is a perfect example of how I was still eating from the fruit of the tree of the knowledge of good and evil instead of the fruit of life from God's spirit. I loved to relax after a long day and have a drink or two; it became a habit. Deep inside, I would feel like it was time to stop, and suddenly my mind would be at war with this feeling, saying things like, "That is not God's voice, because almost every prophet in the Bible would drink wine. Even Noah grew a vineyard when he got out of the ark." And it would continue like this. My mind would continue to give me more scriptures about how it was OK. This is an example of the battle I spoke of earlier in this book that, when God speaks to you, everything you have learned from your past will immediately try to kill those words from God with everything it can—even by using scripture. The Devil even did this to Jesus out in the wilderness.

Praise the Lord that God is good and extremely patient. As I continued my inner battle, I would say things to myself such as, "If God was so against drinking, He would have said something to Noah, and Jesus's first miracle would not have been providing more wine for a huge wedding party." It can be so easy for the enemy to twist scripture in your mind so that you feel justified going against what God is personally telling you. For six years, every time I would feel the Holy Spirit tell me to stop drinking, I would either agree and try to stop for a while, maybe making it a week on my own strength, before going back to the same thoughts above and deciding that I needed a break and to "relax."

Then one day, I was sitting in the third row of one of my best friends' church. Understand, I was raised in all types of churches, and even my parents had owned one of the largest Bible bookstores, meaning I had the privilege to meet almost every famous Christian author there was. This means that going to church was a routine for me, and I have seen many different preaching styles that included different ways of getting the congregation to participate more and get them more involved.

So while sitting in the third row of his church, he said, "Anyone who feels that they have not fully done the will of God, or has fallen short, please stand up, and let us pray together." Immediately my mind rebelled, thinking, *Well, who has not missed it? Because everyone does.* Everyone stood up, including my wife and three daughters next to me. But I refused, thinking that I was not going to be manipulated like that. In retrospect, I should have stood out of sheer respect for my friend, who was right in front of us, however, my pride refused to let me. As I sat there, I reached out to God, asking if I was missing it and coming up short. God said to me, "No, you are not. You are fine. This is not what I want you to hear." This calmed me, and I knew I was OK with God, but my flesh was still fighting and screaming at me to stand up, telling me that my wife was going to be angry at me and trying to guilt me by telling me I was setting a "bad" example for my children. The flesh screamed in my head to stand up, but I refused, because I knew that the still, small voice of God had told me I was OK.

When everyone sat back down, the pastor went on to preach on Gideon, specifically Judges 6:11: "Then the angel of the Lord came and sat under the oak that was in Ophrah, which belonged to Joash the Abiezrite as his son Gideon was beating out wheat in the wine press in order to save it from the Midianites." At first I thought he was taking the verse completely out of context when he said that it is because of the wine that Florida is having so much trouble with hurricanes. Right at this moment, the Holy Spirit spoke to me, saying, "This is what I wanted you to hear." Once again my mind and emotions immediately went on the defensive, reminding me of different scriptures that "proved" that this had nothing to do with drinking. For the next hour, this battle raged inside of me to the point where I did not hear anything else the pastor said, because my mind was preoccupied with tearing that small voice apart, using the scriptures.

For the rest of the day, I was in turmoil over what had taken place in church. God's voice was so direct, completely bringing to life Hebrews 4:12: "For the word of God is living and active and sharper than any two-edged sword, and piercing as far as the division of soul and spirit, of both joints and marrow, and able to judge the thoughts and intentions of the heart." I was troubled on the inside. That evening, like every other evening, I took our dog out on a walk as a time when I could commune with the Lord in peace and uninterrupted quiet. During this walk, God was finally able to get through all of the thoughts and stress inside of me, telling me to just forget about it for now and just spend time with Him this evening. Once I calmed down, quieting my mind and spirit, the Lord said, "Why do you think I came and set everyone free from sin?" I told Him that it was because You wanted to make us Your disciples. God answered saying, "No, that is not why. It was so you could be just like Jesus." I stopped walking. *Just like Jesus?* I had never thought of it like that. God continued, saying, "The goal is to remove your flesh, getting it out of the way in order to let Him live through you." I was amazed and kept imagining what it would be like to have Jesus living completely in me, not myself, and not just being a *follower* of Christ but *just like* Jesus himself. Jesus, who is Lord of all Lords, and King of all Kings, wants to live through us.

I thought on this for a while, still in the flesh and using my worldly mind. I built up pride in the fact of not just being a follower or disciple but having the rights and privileges Jesus had, totally full of the Holy Spirit and Power. Once again God spoke to me, "Do you know the scriptures where Jesus would visit with the people in the bars, made wine, and did not rebuke people who did?" I replied *Yes* and was excited, thinking this is where I would finally get approval to drink alcohol. God continued, "You now also know that I want you to be like Christ here on this Earth." He gave me the scripture Galatians 2:20, which reads, "I have been crucified with Christ; and it is no longer I who live, but Christ lives in me; and the life which I now live in the flesh I live by faith in the Son of God, who loved me and gave Himself up for me." At this point, I fully agreed with God on what He was saying to me, and I was expecting some sort of power, equivalent to what Jesus had, to suddenly fill me.

The Holy Spirit continued, saying, "Let's assume that there is a massive party happening in heaven right now, and remember that you are not your own, but Christ's, right?" I agreed, once again excited for not only my free pass to drinking but also for me to be filled with the same power as Jesus. But God continued asking, "Well, if all of this is true, what did Jesus say at the last supper?" He reminded me of Matthew 26:29, where Jesus says, "But I say to you, I will not drink of this fruit of the vine from now on until that day when I drink it new with you in My Father's kingdom." I stood silently for a while until God said, "Think about it: You are supposed to be the same as Jesus. That is the goal, and even Jesus, who is now in paradise, is not drinking any wine until we are all back together at the end of this age." To be honest, my first thought was *Wow, God—you would be a great lawyer!* Secondly, I was convicted and found that the Lord was absolutely right. I repented and agreed with God.

That night, I promised the Lord to never drink again until, like Jesus, we were all together in heaven. But, to be honest, I maybe made it a week or two before once again breaking down. It took me around 12 years, setback after setback, to finally break free from this stronghold. Many of you may be thinking, "If I knew how to hear from the Lord that clearly, I would have listened and obeyed right away." I warn you against this thought pattern, however. So often when people overcome something with Christ or receive a gift from Him, they quickly turn and use it to judge others and hold them to their new, "holier" standards. Remember that we are not meant to judge. That is God's role, and using knowledge and gifts from Christ to judge and demean others is harmful not only to them but also to yourself, as it builds your pride until it also separates you from God. I'm not justifying my sins as correct, but understand that God has a timeline set for every single one of us, and whether it takes one day or twenty years, as long as we are working with God to accomplish what He sets before us, He is pleased.

One of the hardest setbacks we have to deal with is when we are sick or broke because we do not have enough faith. When we feel as though we are failing, we almost automatically go back to using our worldly minds to do something about it. But this is actually where we need Jesus the most. If we were able to do it by ourselves, then we would not need Jesus. Do not let the many doctrines that churches teach in this world separate you from the fact that you need only Jesus. They will try to tell you that, if you pray longer, fast more, and give more, you will receive more blessings from God. It is Jesus, and only Jesus, who can give you the help you need, and the only thing you need to do in order to receive these blessing is to believe and walk with Him, by the Spirit.

In Mark 11:22–25, after Peter points out to Jesus that a fig tree He had cursed was dead, Jesus said, "Have faith in God. Truly I say to you, whoever says to this mountain, 'Be taken up and cast into the sea,' and does not doubt in his heart, but believes that what he says is going to happen, it will be granted to him. Therefore I say to you, all things for which you pray and ask, believe that you have received them, and they will be granted to you. Whenever you stand praying, forgive, if you have anything against anyone, so that your Father who is in heaven will also forgive your transgressions." The catch in this chapter is that verse 26 says, "But if you do not forgive, neither will your Father who is in heaven forgive your transgression." This is the verse many churches and pastors attach to, saying that God will punish you if you do not get your act together by yourself first. There are many debates about if verse 26 of this chapter is supposed to be in the Bible, because it is not found in many of the early versions of the Bible, and it does not seem to fit in line with everything else God says in His Word. It is not up to you to go off by yourself, without God, finding all the hidden sin and fixing it yourself before going to God. Rather, God wants us to come to Him as we are, so that He can help fix us. We were never meant to walk this road alone.

Always go back to the cornerstone of your trust in God: that God loves you and has saved you through Jesus Christ. "8For by grace you have been saved through faith; and that not of yourselves, it is the gift of God; 9not as a result of works, so that no one may boast." (Ephesians 2:8–9). It is God who gives us faith, through His grace, because of how much He loves you. It is a gift, a free gift, that He gives to us, not because we use our brain to force Him to or because of the sacrifices that we decide to make. When people use scripture to argue against God, they are really telling you that you can treat God as a slave, that you can go to God with a scripture you found in the Bible and demand Him to perform it. Then if He does not, it gives you permission to call God a liar. This is not how we were designed to commune with God; communing with God means having a relationship.

It is also common to hear people switch from having faith *in* God to having the faith *of* God. See the difference? When they say to "have the faith of God," they often add that it is because we are created in His image that we are able to say anything we want. If we believe it, then we will have it, because we are His children, and this is how we should be operating in this world, their reasoning goes. This thinking is a perfect example of how deeply the Devil has been able to twist the word of God in the minds of those who do not hear God for themselves. Jesus said in John 5:19, "Truly, truly, I say to you, the Son can do nothing of Himself, unless it is something He sees the Father doing; for whatever the Father does, these things the Son also does in like manner." And in John 8:28, Jesus says, "When you lift up the Son of Man, then you will know that I am He, and I do nothing on My own initiative, but I speak these things as the Father taught Me." If Jesus was able to do only what the Father showed him to do, why do we think that we can demand anything we want and that God must give it to us?

In Mark 11:22–25, written above, Jesus says, "²³Whoever says to this mountain, 'Be taken up and cast into the sea,' and does not doubt in his heart, but believes that what he says is going to happen, it will be granted to him." Pastors will often equate the mountain in this verse to anything that stands in your way for whatever you want. But understand that, even if it were Jesus who was casting the mountain into the sea, it would only be because the Spirit of God was asking Him to do it, not simply because he wanted that mountain thrown into the sea.

It is true that you receive what you pray for, when it is in line with the will of God. Prayer is not going to God and telling Him what you need, how you need it, and when it needs to happen. In the Greek, the word for prayer is *proseuchomai*, which means "to exchange wishes, to interact with the Lord by switching human wishes or ideas for His wishes as He imparts faith" (Strong's Numbers 4336, Greek). Real faith is going to God in prayer, laying out your problems before Him, and then waiting and listening for what He has to say to you about what to do or say. Real faith is God speaking directly to you, and once you receive His word inside of you, then you have the faith to accomplish whatever it is He has asked you do to. This is why, in Mark 11:23, Jesus says, "and does not doubt in his heart, but believes that what he says is going to happen, it will be granted to him." We must believe what God has spoken inside of us, into our spirit or heart. It is then that we can feel, without question, that, when we speak what God has spoken to us, it will come to pass.

CHAPTER TWELVE

FREEDOM

Lack Nothing

I was spending time with the Lord one morning, and He reminded me of Genesis 24:63: "Isaac went out to meditate in the field toward evening; and he lifted up his eyes and looked, and behold, camels were coming." The Lord was trying to teach me that Isaac had a place to go where he would meditate. To meditate means to "think deeply or focus one's mind for a period of time, in silence or with the aid of chanting, for religious or spiritual purposes as a method of relaxation." (*Webster's Dictionary*). When God first pointed this out, my mind, once again, went on the defensive. I had always been taught that meditation is witchcraft, new age, etc. After this rant in my mind, the Lord said this to me: "You are a spirit, and this is where power comes from. Do you not know that the Devil takes what is mine and distorts it? The way you are looking at meditation is through the distorted eyes of Satan and what you have been taught. But meditating with Me is what I created you for and how we communicate together." In reality, I had been "meditating" all along, which is really what prayer is, but God wanted me to go deeper into His presence by meditating *with Him*. At first, I mentally and verbally prayed for my mind and heart to be covered by the blood of Jesus to ensure that I was not being influenced unwarily by the Devil. Once my mind and spirit were calm, I asked the lord to show me more examples of this in the Bible.

God led me to several scriptures before showing me Psalms 1:2: "But his delight is in the law of the Lord, and in His law he meditates day and night." The first chapter of Psalms has been one of my favorite chapters for a long time, yet I had never seen the word "meditate" in the verse in the light of how the Lord was now showing it to me. This is another great example of how, as we read the Bible, God's word, He will highlight different words or verses to you. When this happens, it is because He wants to teach you something from it. So when this happens, when the words almost come alive off the page to you, stop and meditate with God on those areas.

Next, God directed me to Psalms 19:14: "Let the words of my mouth and the meditation of my heart be acceptable in Your sight, O Lord, my rock and my Redeemer." And then to Psalms 63:6: "When I remember You on my bed, I meditate on You in the night watches." Along with these verses, there were many more that spoke of meditating with God, speaking of it as a positive thing. It shows that we are, indeed, a spirit and that what we let our mind dwell on, or fantasize about, causes our mind and body to follow. Your body is following what you have been meditating on, and we have to meditate on what God has spoken to us to the point of feeling it in our spirit. This will lead to us being able to break our old patterns of behavior and habits.

After I personally accepted this, God asked me to start confessing His words, saying, "He is my source." He also asked me to say out loud, each day on my drive to and from work, that "In Christ I am rich, and I am wealthy." Being a father of three and owning a growing business always had me stressed about money. Stress was all that I thought about, or meditated on. Remember that this is what God asked me to do during this time to deal with the stress I was feeling over money. The Lord will tell you what He wants you to say or do to deal with any issues you may be having in your life. You must hear the words from God and act on what He has specifically told you for this to work for you. I agreed with God to say these things out loud, thinking it would be easy to do. However, driving to work the next day proved otherwise. While I was driving, God spoke to me, saying, "Are you going to say what I told you?" I had completely forgotten. I turned off the radio and said out loud, "I am rich." I stopped; even though I was alone in the car and often sang along to songs on the radio, it felt so stupid to be saying this out loud to myself. But after I said it once, my emotions and mind immediately jumped in, making me think that I was being stupid and that this was embarrassing, almost convincing me to think I was speaking words of sin. I maybe spoke what God told me to six or seven times during the thirty-minute drive to work, and not at all on the drive back home. I justified myself, saying that I had a lot of "real-world" things on my mind to think about.

I share this with you because, while we all have different personalities, at our core we are all the same, and every step of growing in Christ has the same challenges. Colossians 2:6 reads, "Therefore as you have received Christ Jesus the Lord, so walk in Him." Remember how we first received Jesus Christ as Lord? It is always the same pattern: Our hearts say "Yes," but our emotions and mind will give us every reason why we should not do it. It is up to us to believe our hearts and break through our mind and emotions to trust the Lord. The Devil's last attempt to keep you from God is always fear, sometimes fear so strong you feel as though you are unable to move. But remember that we have power and authority over Satan through Jesus Christ. Romans 10:8–11 says, "But what does it say? '⁸The word is near you, in your mouth and in your heart'—that is, the word of faith which we are preaching, ⁹that if you confess with your mouth Jesus as Lord, and believe in your heart that God raised Him from the dead, you will be saved; ¹⁰for with the heart a person believes, resulting in righteousness, and with the mouth he confesses, resulting in salvation. ¹¹For the scripture says, 'Whoever believes in Him will not be disappointed.'"

So the next day, when I was driving to work, it became a little bit easier to say, and by day four, I was easily saying it the entire drive to work and back. On the fifth day, God stopped me and asked me to actually listen to what I was saying. He reminded me of Exodus 3:13–14: "Then Moses said to God, 'Behold, I am going to the sons of Israel, and I will say to them,

'The God of your fathers has sent me to you.' Now they may say to me, 'What is His name?' What shall I say to them?' God said to Moses, 'I AM WHO I AM'; and He said, 'Thus you shall say to the sons of Israel, 'I AM has sent me to you.'" Suddenly I saw the reason God had me saying each day, "I am rich. I am wealthy." It hit me—it was not my fleshly body that was rich and wealthy; rather, it is the "I AM," God who lives inside of me, who is. The Holy Spirit in me is the rich and wealthy one, not me, but when I speak out loud what God is telling me, I join with the Holy Spirit and get to partake of the same riches that the Holy Spirit has. It was such an incredible revelation that caused so much joy in me that I sang praises to the Lord the rest of the drive.

It is amazing when God reveals deep truths to us personally. But the real test comes when we have to apply what we've learned. This came for me later that night, when I was out walking my dog and I thought about how the Lord was leading my youngest daughter and me towards having her attend a university that would cost at least $60,000 a year. I become so stressed with thoughts of money that I could not hear God clearly on anything He wanted me to do concerning extra expenses. But even with this, I kept getting feelings out of the blue that she was to go to this specific university. It was a deep, inner thought that would randomly interrupt my everyday thoughts and desires. This is one good way to know that it is God speaking to you. If the feeling or thoughts keep coming up even though they do not make sense to your brain, and they align with the Bible, then you can be sure it is from God.

Remember that just that morning, I had the revelation that the God who lives inside of me is rich and wealthy, and not even eight hours later, when He brought up this university, I claimed that it was not from Him and started using the knowledge the world had taught me, arguing that there was no way I was going to be able to pay that much for her school.

The stress over this built and built until God finally broke through my internal loud thoughts and directed me to Matthew 6:19–24, where Jesus says,

> "¹⁹Do not store up for yourselves treasures on earth, where moth and rust destroy, and where thieves break in and steal. ²⁰But store up for yourselves treasures in heaven, where neither moth nor rust destroys, and where thieves do not break in or steal; ²¹for where your treasure is, there your heart will be also. ²²The eye is the lamp of the body; so then if your eye is clear, your whole body will be full of light. ²³But if your eye is bad, your whole body will be full of darkness. If then the light that is in you is darkness, how great is the darkness! ²⁴No one can serve two masters; for either he will hate the one and love the other, or he will be devoted to one and despise the other. You cannot serve God and wealth."

I had always thought the last verse of this scripture never made sense in the context of the rest of the verses. However, when I was stressing about paying for this university, God directed me to this scripture and revealed to me that I had been looking at it all wrong. He explained to me that we are not meant to take refuge in the god of money and that doing so is idolatry. Instead, we are meant to do the opposite, taking refuge in God and what He says, while trusting Him to bring in the money for what He asks us to do. Fully coming to terms with this was not easy. I had a lot of old mental thoughts and feelings to work through and give up to God. Giving up your old ways can hurt, but, in the end, it is always worth it.

Once Christ won the battle inside of me, even though I did not find a suitcase full of money on the ground that night, I found something better. I found God, and He opened up to me so many scriptures that I had read in the past but never fully understood. One of these was Proverbs 8:11: "For wisdom is better than jewels; and all desirable things cannot compare with her." God's wisdom is better than gold, silver, or rubies. God explained that wisdom from Him is not found in textbooks but rather in hearing His Spirit talk with you. This turned into weeks of going through all the scriptures on wisdom and seeing what an advantage King David had by pursuing God and His wisdom above everything else. David knew that listening to God was the reason for his success and glory on this Earth. He understood that God is good. I eventually settled it in my heart that I was going to be able to send my daughter to this university. But, instead of trying to do it in my own strength, I was going to watch in excitement as the Lord blessed my daughter with the ability to go there because of His love for us.

During this time, I did not just throw the wisdom and understanding that God was giving at that moment out the window because I did not understand it. Many Christians will do this, whether on purpose or accidentally. They let the emotions and "logical" world thinking hold them back from God's blessings. Even though that evening I did not have the money to send my daughter to that school, I knew that I would because it was God who was telling me that I would. However, life is not as simple as having a thought and making it an action; there are countless thoughts, emotions, decisions, and outside sins hitting us every day. This is why, in 1 Thessalonians 5:16–19, Paul says, "[16]Rejoice always; [17]pray without ceasing; [18]in everything give thanks; for this is God's will for you in Christ Jesus. [19]Do not quench the Spirit." We have to do our best each and every day to be in tune with God in all we do. King David understood this and in Psalms 18:34–35 says, "[34]He trains my hands for battle, so that my arms can bend a bow of bronze. [35]You have also given me the shield of Your salvation, and Your right hand upholds me; and Your gentleness makes me great." When King David heard a command from God, he did not simply sit back and relax, expecting it to just happen without himself doing anything. Instead, he understood that, every day, all the things he did were for the good of the kingdom and that he could not just make the decision to do nothing and let God do it on His own. Instead, he worked with God each step of the way.

When we go off and work in our own strength, even if God originally spoke for something to happen, it will not happen if we do not work with God along the way. We cannot blame God when it doesn't come to pass if we tried to do it independently from Him. Many Christians fall into this trap when they believe that just because they accepted Christ, anything bad that happens to them after that moment is God's fault. But we know this is not true. When we walk independently from God, it is our fault when things end up poorly. It is hard to fully crucify our flesh and let God's will be fully done with us, and it takes our whole life of working with God each and every day. However, with each victory, it becomes easier to win the next battle. Eventually God brings us into deeper understanding as we wage larger and larger battles. Remember that the battles that God asks us to wage come from hearing His voice and His voice being supported by scripture. It is not finding a scripture for yourself and then deciding that you can accomplish it on your own strength. When God speaks to you, you will know it, and you will need His help, grace, and wisdom to accomplish it.

Another good scripture on wisdom is Proverbs 8:12: "I am wisdom, and I have good judgment. I also have knowledge and good sense" (New Century Version). This is a great verse if you begin second-guessing yourself. For example, with my daughter's university I spoke of earlier, when the Holy Spirit told me to stop looking at the money as a god but rather trust fully in His voice, I did not just accept it and then start spending money on anything I wanted. Rather, I came humbly before the Lord, thanking him and waiting on every decision that I could, including how to handle employees, how to invest and grow the business, how and when to travel, and everything else that I could. Even though, once in a while, I would stress over the money, I would always go back to God and give those worries to Him. Eventually, everything began to fall into place, and the Lord blessed me so that I was able to pay for my daughter to go to the university He had led her and I toward months before.

Do not be fooled—sin is always with us, waiting for us to slip up as it crouches at the door. It waits for anytime you begin to doubt or question God to jump in and push us further away from Him. This is seen in Genesis 4:7: "If you do well, will not your countenance be lifted up? And if you do not do well, sin is crouching at the door; and its desire is for you, but you must master it." The battle with sin is constant, and never ends. This battle can also be seen in the New Testament.

"⁴He did this so that we could be the kind of people the law correctly wants us to be. Now we do not live following our sinful selves, but we live following the Spirit. ⁵Those who live following their sinful selves think only about things that their sinful selves want. But those who live following the Spirit are thinking about the things the Spirit wants them to do. ⁶If people's thinking is controlled by the sinful self, there is death. But if their thinking is controlled by the Spirit, there is life and peace. ⁷When people's thinking is controlled by their sinful selves, they are against God, because they refuse to obey God's law and really are not even able to obey God's law. ⁸Those

people who are ruled by their sinful selves cannot please God. ⁹But you are not ruled by your sinful selves. You are ruled by the Spirit if that Spirit of God really lives in you. But the person who does not have the Spirit of Christ does not belong to Christ. ¹⁰Your body will always be dead because of sin. But if Christ is in you, then the Spirit gives you life, because Christ made you right with God. ¹¹God raised Jesus from the dead, and if God's Spirit is living in you, he will also give life to your bodies that die. God is the One who raised Christ from the dead, and he will give you life through his Spirit that lives in you. ¹²So, my brothers and sisters, we must not be ruled by our sinful selves or live the way our sinful selves want. ¹³If you use your lives to do the wrong things your sinful selves want, you will die spiritually. But if you use the Spirit's help to stop doing the wrong things you do with your body, you will have true life. ¹⁴The true children of God are those who let God's Spirit lead them."

—Romans 8:4–12

(New Century Version)

The verses above are a great example about the freedom in Christ. As we walk with Him, listening to His Spirit inside of us and acting on it, we realize that He always knows best, and we get better at controlling our mind and emotions. You will find that you actually start looking forward to watching God come through for you, which builds your hope. Once your hope is strong, you are ready for the next step with God.

Patience becomes exciting for you, because, as James 1:2–4 says, "²Consider it all joy, my brethren, when you encounter various trials, ³knowing that the testing of your faith produces endurance (patience). ⁴And let endurance (patience) have its perfect result, so that you may be perfect and complete, lacking in nothing."

And lacking in nothing is God's will for us.

Hallelujah.

ACKNOWLEDGMENTS

I would like to give a big thank-you and hug to my wife, Barbara. For 28 years, she has seen all my shortcomings but still believes in my making our family decisions based on hearing from the voice of God. That has got to be the toughest job of all—being close to someone so imperfect but watching as God uses such a person to make His words come to pass.

To all my Daughters, Lindsey, Kaela, and Serena, who, by observing how we lived, believed, and learned, came to hear the voice of the Lord themselves and walk in it. It truly is the biggest reward of our life.

And finally, a super-special thank-you to my daughter Kaela. I cannot acknowledge her enough. Without her editing this book before I sent it to the editors, I believe the professional editors would have just sent it back to me, saying the challenge was too hard. God is good. As I finished the second draft, I decided to go through it again, a third time, adding more personal stories. But the Lord stopped me and asked me to ask my daughter Kaela if she wouldn't mind proofing it for me.

She agreed, but after three days, she came downstairs with just four pages in her hands. I thought she should have been done by then; a couple of missing commas, a few misspelled words—I mean, *How hard could it be?* But, to my horror, the four pages were highlighted in four different colors with so many mistakes that she didn't know where to begin.

Well, after overcoming my wounded pride and some negotiating, she agreed to finish it so that I could send it to the editors and not be too embarrassed. Kaela worked tirelessly for three months. I would see her late at night just working away. That's commitment.

So basically, this book was written by two people—which reminds me of the scripture in 2 Corinthians 13:1: "Every fact is to be confirmed by the testimony of two or three witnesses." So, we have myself and my daughter Kaela; and our prayer is that, after reading these pages, you will be the third.

ABOUT THE
AUTHOR

Ed Carpenter was raised in a family that ran one of the Top 25 Christian book and music stores in the United States. This gave him the opportunity to cross paths with many famous Christian authors and singers over many years. After college, Ed left his comfortable boyhood life and went on a mission trip to connect with the Holy Spirit and tune into the voice of God. This challenging quest for faith preceded a successful business and family, sharing the knowledge of how to hear God with his wife and three daughters. Since semi-retiring and hearing the Lord ask him to help others hear His word, he has written this book.